Overcoming Depression

Books to change your life and work.
Accessible, easy to read and easy to act on –
other titles in the **How To** series include:

Self-Counselling
How to develop the skills to positively manage your life

Achieving Personal Well-being
How to discover and balance your physical and emotional needs

Using Relaxation for Health and Success
Stress reducing techniques for confidence and positive health

Controlling Anxiety
How to master fears and phobias and start living with confidence

Thrive on Stress
Manage pressure and positively thrive on it

The **How To** Series now contains
around 200 titles in the following categories:

Business & Management
Career Choices
Career Development
Computers & the Net
Creative Writing
Home and Family
Living & Working Abroad
Personal Development
Personal Finance
Self-Employment & Small Business
Study Skills & Student Guides

Send for a free copy of the latest catalogue:

How To Books
Customer Services Dept.
Plymbridge Distributors Ltd, Estover Road
Plymouth PL6 7PY, United Kingdom
Tel: 01752 202301   Fax: 01752 202331
http://www.howtobooks.co.uk

Overcoming Depression

*Get rid of depression using
this practical two-part programme*

DEAN JUNIPER

How To Books

Published by How To Books Ltd,
3 Newtec Place, Magdalen Road,
Oxford OX4 1RE, United Kingdom.
Tel: (01865) 793806. Fax: (01865) 248780.
email: info@howtobooks.co.uk
http://www.howtobooks.co.uk

British Library Cataloguing in Publication Data.
A catalogue record for this book is available from
the British Library.

Edited by Francesca Mitchell
Cover design by Shireen Nathoo Design
Cover image by PhotoDisc
Cover copy by Sallyann Sheridan

Produced for How To Books by Deer Park Productions
Typeset by Kestrel Data, Exeter
Printed and bound by Cromwell Press, Trowbridge, Wiltshire

NOTE: The material contained in this book is set out in good
faith for general guidance and no liability can be accepted
for loss or expense incurred as a result of relying in particular
circumstances on statements made in the book. The laws and
regulations are complex and liable to change, and readers should
check the current position with the relevant authorities before
making personal arrangements.

Contents

Preface

We live in an epoch of growing personal crisis in which con-
temporary Capitalism has clearly slipped its chain, and is now
at the throat of the world. In response, governments of every
political stripe are at one in emphasising the minimalist character
of their roles. They proclaim impotence as a strength, and preach
the paradoxical virtues of incessant change and beneficent insecurity. As market forces, then, increasingly determine values
and competitive frenzy grows, unchecked by democratic or auto-
cratic control, so stresses on individuals will increase, and they will
fall prey to a variety of ailments, amongst which depression and
apathy will figure prominently. Their sole chance of psychological
survival in the emotional and cognitive domains will be to build
their own ego-strength by systematic discovery and reinforcement
of intimate self-gratifications; no simple task in a milieu intent on
stripping them of human dignity, and tutoring them in helpless
resignation. Few will be able to accomplish this without some
guidance, and providing a framework for such guidance is the
meaning and purpose of this book.

Dean Juniper

1

Overcoming Depression

YOU ARE NOT ALONE

There is good reason to believe that, despite substantial improvements in physical health and an increase in lifespan, the level of depression in the UK has been rising since the 1950s and may continue to rise. The number of adults consulting their doctors for depression almost doubled during the 1990s. During this period, although the suicide rate did not increase significantly, for every person who succeeded in committing suicide, 20 people made serious attempts on their lives.

THE BACKGROUND

There have been profound changes in our society since the 1950s, characterised by a sharp increase in stress levels. Job security has all but disappeared, as we experience pressure to be 'flexible' in our work. One section of the population is unemployed, while another is overworked. An increased emphasis on competitiveness in work and society has meant that we are constantly experiencing assessment, comparison, devaluation and disparagement. The ever-expanding power of global corporations has led to a feeling of helplessness. People are far more mobile than previously – they no longer expect to spend their lives in the community in which they were born, and thus no longer have the daily support of their extended family and community. The nature of the family has changed, with a growth of one-parent, step- and grandparent families. But perhaps the most dramatic development has been in information technology. We are constantly bombarded with information – from radio, television, mobile phones, and Internet. Even a modern car has a multitude of signals that force themselves on the driver's attention. All this leads to sensory overload, which in turn leads to stress. And stress is a major contributory factor in depression.

But although it is a huge problem, depression afflicts only a minority. Despite stress, the majority are not depressed; they cope, not with hilarity or euphoria, but with a dogged cheerfulness and a dour optimism. And as far as current research reveals, this coping capacity rests on eleven strengths or skills.

People who cope successfully with depression

- Have aims and hopes that are adjusted to *their* personal realities.

- Maintain a steady, other-blame, credit balance on their personal responsibility account.

- *Keep up regular programmes of anticipated and realised pleasures.*

- Sift and select what they read, view and hear so as to exclude the demoralising or the morbid.

- Sustain a faith in something or some person outside themselves.

- *Establish and nourish at least one confiding relationship.*

- *Have hobbies, activities, interests and manageable responsibilities.*

- *Preserve healthy rhythms of sleeping, eating, etc.*

- Stay sensitive to their own mood-changes and are quick to react to them with rest, relaxation, recreation or variation.

- Do not carry the sins of the world on their shoulders.

- Are orientated to the present and future, and do not dwell on the past.

Unwrapping the list

First we should be clear that none of those items holds priority in successful coping; it is simply a comprehensive list based on the coping experience of people in general. As far as individuals are concerned, a pick-and-mix of selected items and a concentration on a small number is likely to be the pattern for coping successfully.

But that does not mean that the list is not useful. Quite the contrary is the case; you can tease out *many essential coping techniques from it* and, if you are suffering from depression, you can put your own pick-and-mix coping plan together.

The aim of this book

- To give you insight into the workings of your depression without bogging you down with causes and origins.

- To point out a range of possibilities for gaining control over a depression, and suggest an overall strategy.

- To provide you with tactics for controlling thinking and behaviour which are designed to lift depressive moods.

- To help you summon up and organise your resources so as to maximise their compensatory and pleasure-giving possibilities.

- To guard against the long-term consequences of depression on life-chances.

- To help you find ways of staying depression-free in future.

2

What is Depression?

Depression is an emotional illness with variable low moods that occasionally become more positive, and sometimes excited or cheerful. Depressive thinking is characteristically gloomy, defeatist, self-derogatory and preoccupied with the past. Problems loom large in depressions, and depressives are often tormented by self-designated duties or responsibilities. Clear, creative, decisive thinking is also frequently impaired, energy levels are low, and a range of physical ailments may be triggered or intensified.

IS DEPRESSION A SEPARATE ILLNESS?

It's useful to regard depression as the largest and commonest emotional ailment amongst a range which also includes anxiety and compulsion. Although each can exist separately and, in some rare instances, even appear to be in tight compartments, there is usually a degree of overlap. It is, for instance, common to find some measure of depression in those who are tied to the rituals and impulses of compulsive behaviour. Depressives can, and often do, suffer from anxiety. And the concept of a broad ailment is a useful one to hold, if for no other reason than that it serves to indicate that there is a common cognitive-behavioural approach to all three.

HOW DEEP IS YOUR DEPRESSION?

Though depressions come in varying degrees of depth and length, they are often longstanding, moderately troubling, states which make life seem pointless or trivial. If you agree with the majority of the following statements about yourself, then you are probably suffering from a mild to moderate depression.

- Secretly you are sorry you were ever born.

- When you look back on your life it seems a succession of crises and struggles.

- You are easily hurt.

- There is always some relationship or other coming apart.

- There is always a huge gap between what you want and what you are.

- There is always something to depress or worry you.

- You deny you are guilty, but your thoughts and actions reflect little else.

- You find the prospect of death a little thrilling or, at least, a kind of solution.

- Most common life-satisfactions seem to you overrated, but you cannot do without them.

- Secretly, you despise everybody, yourself included.

You are also probably still within reach of the type of self-managed help that this book offers and, if you let yourself work within its systematic betterment programmes, there should be sustained benefits for you.

But depressions can be significantly deeper than mild to moderate. They can reduce mental and physical efficiency to levels of virtual half-functioning. If you agree with the majority of the following statements, then you have moved into the severest category of depression.

- You often feel tempted to stay in bed all day. There seems no point in getting up and dressed.

- Eating meals has become simply a chore, and you know you are undernourished.

- You find it hard to concentrate for more than a short period. Conversations fade in and out.

- It feels a huge effort just to walk about. As for going to work, this is almost impossible (or is impossible).

- Starting conversations is extremely difficult. It feels as if your lips are frozen. It is an effort to speak.

- The nagging need to escape to the safety of your bed asserts itself in work or in social events.

- Feelings of contentment or pleasure (if they occur at all) are very short-lived and are soon blanketed by moods of despair or bitterness.

- Fatigue and exhaustion are with you continuously, even at the moment of waking. Sleep is difficult to attain and maintain.

- Often you weep but usually only when you are alone.

- Irritation with other people increases. You make angry asides under your breath.

If you have agreed with most of the above statements, this book can certainly help you, but not on its own. Your safest, most reliable, but not necessarily easiest course is to seek professional aid. You have a legal right to ask your doctor to refer you to a clinical psychologist for a diagnosis and a therapeutic recommend-ation. This may be difficult. Your doctor may not want to refer you. Insist on it; *if necessary change your doctor or see another partner*, but make sure you get professional help.

SUPPOSE DEPRESSION IS NOT YOUR PROBLEM

It could be that you are indeed suffering, but not from depression. If you agree with the majority of the following statements about yourself, then you are not depressed but anxious, and anxious in a particularly tormenting way about your health.

- You have a new stress symptom again. It does not make you feel ill. It may not be present as you wake up, but it tends to reappear as soon as you are fully awake.

- Like previous symptoms, it *could* be a symptom of a serious physical or mental disease, but you guess that this is not the case.

- Almost nobody close shares your concern. You seem well enough to others.

- This new symptom is ruling the roost as usual. All previous ones have disappeared in its presence.

- This symptom has followed on another closely. But sometimes there can be a gap of months or years.

- This symptom has developed rapidly. Unlike some of the others, it was not triggered by an unaccustomed shock or experience.

- You will check the symptom with the doctor. But you are almost certain that no physical cause will be found.

- This symptom is not a repeater, e.g. one you have had before. Repeaters tend to be weaker.

- You expect the symptom to persist for weeks or months.

- You've reached the conclusion that the symptom-chain is a kind of life-style.

This not especially common condition is called hypochondria, and is capable of destroying a sufferer's enjoyment of life almost completely. But with skilled professional help it can be eased considerably.

Perhaps you have a compulsive illness
Suppose, however, you affirm the majority of these statements:

- You are forever constructing lists of matters to remember, as a means of lowering anxiety about forgetting.

- You are consumed with impotent rage towards other people, triggered by harmless remarks or actions.

- You are continuously preoccupied with your clothes and physical appearance. Anxiety, annoyance, even rage over some trivial flaw in hair, make-up or clothes can poison your mood.

- Personal hygiene obsesses you. Your body must be cleaned according to strict rituals. All body odours must be removed or concealed.

- Superstitious behaviour controls your life. This ranges from avoiding cracks in the pavements, to drawing curtains to prevent sunlight falling on your body.

- Your hobbies become obsessive; for example an interest

in model railways compels you to try to duplicate a real time-table, exactly.

- You desire full environmental control and are very intolerant of disorder; for instance you line up the family shoes according to size, colour, style; you place books, papers or other objects at right angles to the furniture on which they rest, etc.

- Rituals of many kinds dominate you. They may involve cooking, eating, washing, security, etc.

- You find taking decisions very difficult or, having made them, you are tormented with doubts.

- Your personal relationships lack spontaneity. You are forever examining your feelings or contriving warmth.

If so, you are seriously obsessive – possibly to the extent that your whole life and the lives of others around you are being ruined by futile, inescapable, self-imposed regulation. Again, you certainly need professional help for a condition of this kind, but again there will be a significant element of self-management (exercises and practice you do on your own) required in any therapy you may receive.

WHY GO IN FOR THIS DIAGNOSIS?

First, we need to make the objectives of this book realistic and clear. This is vital because the term depression is often slackly assigned; it has been so popularised and often trivialised as to be virtually stripped of meaning. This book has specific targets which are very meaningful, and it would be irresponsible to raise the hopes of those either not suffering from depression or too depressed to profit from its programme without support. At the same time we need to take the opportunity to empower readers who have conditions other than depression to seek appropriate help. And because the programmes in this book are built on clear-thinking and systematic exercises, we need to establish a similar routine for all those who hope to make use of them.

Going further than diagnosis

We shall, of course, have to go further than diagnosis if you intend to use this book. It will be necessary to explore the possible causes of depression and provide some background to reinforce the effectiveness of the suggested programmes. Going further means introducing fresh concepts, the most immediate of which are stress and coping.

UNDERSTANDING STRESS

In the previous chapter we identified some of the most recently applied pressures of living in the modern world. Some of these are new or, at any rate, newly reintroduced. But these also exist alongside traditional stress-inducing factors which are very much the products of societies that are divorced from natural living and behaving.

Depression and stress

What is the relationship between depression and stress? It is not a simple one. Stress is the consequence of being put under strong pressure and not allowed either to avoid or fight it. The experience of being in this position is termed stressful, and is felt as anxiety, tension or various bodily symptoms such as headache or skin complaints. But there is a very primitive third stress position, neither flight nor fight, which may be produced by persistent circumstances of strain. This is like the immobile frozen state that trapped animals assume as a natural form of defence. In human beings it is felt as a mood of despair and frustration, without positive position; apathy rather than activity rules. Depression then can be viewed as an outcome, or product, of unresolved stress, which is why, for instance, we introduce techniques of relaxation (much associated with stress-management) as part of a large appendix of this book.

COPING AND FAILING TO COPE

At the close of the previous chapter we introduced the concept of coping and listed individual techniques for avoiding breakdown. As we noted, a majority of people do cope to a greater or lesser degree with the stresses of modern-day living. Although this book is focused on the large minority of non-copers, it is very useful to analyse success, which we can do by listing the responses of good copers to questions about their individual techniques.

Copers' responses

- My coping capability is rooted in an intuition of inevitable challenge (sometime I'm going to need the resources/techniques that I maintain).

- My coping capability is a 'natural possession' (I've always had it, and am grateful for it).

- My coping capability is potentiated by alcohol, smoking or other supports.

- I attribute my coping capability to confident parenting.

- I attribute my coping capability to imitative factors (I've modelled myself on others).

- I attribute my coping capability to will-power.

- I attribute my coping capability to belief in God.

- I am aware that to attribute my coping capability to luck is probably an admission that I do not possess the capability.

- My coping capability is mainly of the desensitising kind (I rehearse potential crises mentally and adjust my reactions to them in advance).

- My coping capability is mainly of the active kind (I throw all my resources into combating the threat).

- My coping capability is mainly of the denying kind (I relabel threats as non-threatening, play-problems instead).

- My coping capability can probably be developed further.

- My coping capability is highly adaptable and I'm confident it can manage a variety of crises.

- I consider that thinking about coping bears a 'happy centipede' risk (raising the level of awareness of it may inhibit its effectiveness).

- My coping capability depends on others' support (I am, of necessity, passed from supportive hand to hand, like a baton in life's relay race).

This is a very interesting and comprehensive list which would take a book three times larger than this one to analyse thoroughly.

We shall, in fact, tackle at least six responses in some detail in the forthcoming chapters and appendices, but for the moment confine ourselves to the last one.

Although it is last on the list, this response is one of the most significant. Those psychologists who attribute depression to a breakdown in socially supportive relationships would say it is *the* significant response. Without going as far as that, this book does emphasise the social factor and consistently recommends that social considerations are an important part of developing coping skills for several of its Action Sites. An Action Site is a specific method of gaining leverage over each of ten aspects of depression, as we shall see in Chapter 5. Social support can, in effect, sharply modify the stresses of life. The research examples are striking, and show the extraordinary supportive power of affection, feelings of belonging or group membership. For example:

- Babies whose mothers go out to work in the second six months of their lives fail to gain toilet control as quickly as those whose mothers are not at work. But after that second six months mothers may go out to work without apparently affecting the baby's development.

- Patients with *myocardial infarction* (heart disease involving inflammation and blockings) progress just as well at home as in hospital despite the differences in terms of the intensive care and specialist equipment that a hospital may provide.

- Women who suffer severe misfortunes and lack good confidential relationships are ten times more likely to be depressed than those who suffer similar misfortunes yet have such relationships, particularly with husbands, partners and relatives.

- Single or divorced men who lose their mothers are nine times more likely to commit suicide than married men.

- Depression is approximately twice as likely among older people who have poor social contacts than among those older people whose social relationships are good.

- People die less frequently in the six months before, than in the six months after, their birthdays most probably because they anticipate the pleasure of the occasion and the satisfaction of the achievement of an acknowledged social event.

A VARIETY OF METHODS

This book's purpose is to identify key methods of coping either indirectly with stress or directly with depression, and by building instructions on these into a self-managed, betterment programme give you a chance to strengthen your defences appropriately.

Returning to the copers' responses, you will have also noticed the third, which spoke of alcohol and other supports, and doubtless you will be thinking of the part that drugs might play in lifting a depression.

Why self-help can be a better option than drugs or even counselling

The reason why successful self-help is so much more effective than drugs or counselling in depression lies less with actual treatment and more with the quality of recovery.

Drugs, especially Prozac, can certainly lift a depression, *but they leave the former sufferer with no understanding of how the trick was accomplished and, more seriously, what other than drugs, may stop the condition recurring.* The dependency situation is obvious.

Counselling too can shift depression, but unless it is much more than simple 'listening ear' therapy and provides a rational explanation for the condition and a future preventive programme, then it too will leave the sufferer with little more than a dependent relationship.

Only successful self-help that promotes sufficient understanding of the condition, combined with a self-discovered treatment strategy and an independent future programme, can help you cope fully.

3

Six Steps for Overcoming Depression

There are six steps to ridding oneself of a depression or, at least, bringing it under an acceptable measure of control:

1. understanding what it takes
2. preparing and planning the programme
3. starting out on the programme
4. keeping going
5. watching how you go
6. motivating yourself.

Although we list them in a seemingly independent series, there is, in fact, a considerable degree of overlap, and the sequence is not precise.

1. UNDERSTANDING WHAT IT TAKES

It would be easy to say that it takes determination but this would be a form of word-evasion. What is determination? Perhaps it is nothing more than a cost-benefit analysis done by the mind on the alternatives of being or not being depressed. So, how does this balancing exercise look? We might begin by listing the basic disadvantages thus:

- Depression reduces personal effectiveness.

- Depression is associated with, if it does not actually cause, physical ill health.

- Depressives run some risk of suicide and a much greater one of attempting it.

- Depression eats into contentment with life and, since life is finite, means a loss of living time.

Of these four, the last is arguably the most serious and the one which should weigh heaviest with any reader of this book. Making up the ledger responsibly, we must also list the advantages, however slim.

- Depression may gain attention and possibly sympathy, but neither is reliable.

- Depression can act as a subtle defence against guilty thinking or traumatic memories, becoming detached from them as possible causes.

- In some creative artists a depressive mood can become a mindset for the production or recovery of material and its shaping in creative terms. This is not true for all artists and not even reliably true for the depressive creative.

The imbalance is obvious, and the advantage of ridding oneself of or gaining control of one's depression is clear. But it is still a considerable step from grasping the issues to deciding to act. Nobody can take that step for another. All that can be done is to lay out the case for action and leave the conclusion to power the result. The rest is down to self-belief.

Believing in oneself
There is, of course, much more to understanding what it takes in terms of determination than a cost-benefit analysis, however carefully made. Hope and faith in oneself are also powerful factors in bringing about intimate change. They may not seem powerful; indeed in the depths of a depression, hope and faith are likely to be faint, weakened by the depression and little to be relied upon for motivation or continuity of purpose. But hope and faith in oneself do not rest on passing whims; they have more lasting aspects which can be uncovered by looking deep inside yourself.

Why you should believe in yourself, despite yourself
Of one thing we can be sure, the individual self is good in itself. It must be because it is the dynamic product of millions of years of quiet but dramatic struggle. Despite all the odds we, and other species, have 'come through'. We are a triumph of biological will and every intricate cellular mechanism within us testifies to this triumph in its duty and devotion. *We are in the presence of a life-force for stability, one which is constantly seeking to maintain the equilibrium of systems within its control and, should they be out*

of balance, to restore them. So, even if we have no conscious hope, a deeper confidence resides within us; and though our faith may be non-existent, myriads of faithful ones keep watch and ward at all points inside us.

2. PREPARING AND PLANNING THE PROGRAMME

This book provides a programme – in other words a framework of future tactics linked to a loose schedule with opportunities to evaluate progress as the programme unfolds. There is preparation and planning involved but, apart from two preliminary provisions, most of what will be required is contained in the material and explained as it is reached.

Ready yourself for some, perhaps much, charting and record-keeping, ensuring that such written work can be kept confidential. And a thorough audit of resources should be made, including items such as: hobbies, activities and interests, explored or un-explored; social facilities, local or regional; relationships, friends and acquaintances; status of finance, dependents; occupational status, satisfactions and prospects; etc. We could call this the positive assets audit, and a second, smaller, negative version might also be useful, summarising such deficits as debts and social no-go areas – anything that may act as a road-block on the way to recovery and need tackling or addressing.

What do I need to consider?

- Have I thoroughly absorbed the message of Chapter 2 and am I clear that this is indeed the programme for me?

- Have I materials to hand for charting and recording purposes?

- What are my current interests?

- What are my past interests?

- Do I have possible future interests?

- Can I list my resources?
  My intimate, supportive, relationships: spouse, partner, child, parent.
  My friends and acquaintances.
  My job and job prospects.
  My financial circumstances.

- What are the local community supports? For example, clubs, associations, leisure centres, educational institutions.

- Are there any serious roadblocks to lifting my depression which may need special negotiation? For example, social isolation, job insecurity, physical ill-health.

3. STARTING OUT ON THE PROGRAMME

When and how should you start? There is no time to lose in starting, but the precise act of beginning is often difficult. Usually it is not a question of deciding to begin; the decision is taken for you by the action of an upswing (a change towards a more optimistic mood). Details of such upswings and how to capitalise on them form an important part of the programme to come. At this point it is sufficient to identify them as significant and flag them for further reading. *The act of beginning is, in fact, highly reinforcing; it is not easy to stop once one has begun.* The fact of beginning also has great influence on point 4 of this list of steps.

4. KEEPING GOING

Once one has begun, some of the effort required to keep going is lessened because the diary and chart-keeping, regular activity-scheduling and several other repetitive features carry the action forward. Additional momentum is provided by any review on your part of distance already covered and improvements won, however small. Indeed the next step, watching how you go, reflects forwards and backwards, and influences both continuity and motivation.

Momentum

Once an object has been set in motion, much less effort is required to keep it moving than was needed to shift it in the first place. Once the initial effort to gain momentum in starting your programme has been made, *only the gentlest of pushes will be required thereafter.*

Keeping going is also very much about organising goals and maintaining a constant, goal-seeking, mindset. The ultimate goal is, of course, to lift the depression that brought us to consider this book in the first place. But though that is a good overall objective, it will be helpful to think continuously about some of the important sub-goals also involved.

Action sites as sub-goals
These leverage points on depression, soon to be explained, represent ten useful goals and, as the Betterment Programme unfolds, there will be a succession of such secondary objectives to aim for.

An even wider objective
Most people believe that *we have but one life, which is not a rehearsal and which will not be repeated. We therefore have no time to waste on depression and an overriding incentive to rid ourselves of it as soon as we can.*

5. WATCHING HOW YOU GO

Various methods of evaluation and self-appraisal are introduced into the programme so that a constant overview of progress can be made. This is vital for sharpening up a personal strategy, and a valuable factor in maintaining momentum.

Developing a charting mindset
While you don't need to become obsessive about it, a reasonably reliable, charting mindset is essential for success in lifting a depression. Try now to think yourself into such a mindset, reminding yourself how vital it is to keep consistent reliable records. Here is some guidance.

Goals, charts and diary-keeping
It's not easy to get a grip on depression by yourself without some use of goals, charts and diaries. Goals (realistic descriptions of what you aim to achieve), charts (methods of continuously recording and assessing progress towards those aims) and diaries (informal daily or weekly jottings) are some of the most powerful improvement tools the self-manager can possess. In a very real sense they are more than tools. Consider their use in tackling the often very troublesome problem of early-waking in depression. A realistic goal to aim for might be the attainment of at least four unbroken nights per week at the end of a three month period.

Now, even at this earliest point of planning, before the design of a chart, the crystallisation of an aim in formal terms begins to have a startling psychological effect. A mindset for change and improvement has been built which, without any further positive action, can cause an immediate improvement. At the very least motivation has been given and the beginnings of momentum made.

There is nothing complex about the design of an appropriate chart. It will need to have recording space for at least six months of nights and a simple visual method of noting early arousals and subsequent sleeping retrievals. Timings can be introduced if you feel they are important. With unbroken lines standing for uninterrupted sleep, a typical chart might look like this.

Record of 14 nights

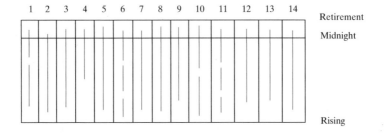

This chart, although not complete, shows improvement and represents a powerful reinforcement as a visual display. On the other hand, if its sleep patterns continued unchanged the reinforcement would focus on the diary with its simultaneous record of events experienced and tactics for better sleeping.

Charts, charting and records – do's and don'ts

- Remember that even very rudimentary charting often seems to generate an improvement in itself.

- Diaries and numerical records are both excellent forms of charting. But combining the two will be even more effective.

- Record everything of significance, but leave space also for what is insignificant.

- Set yourself a recording period – five minutes at the end of the day or 20 at the end of the week.

- Make up your own shorthand and jargon.

- If you want to use grades, A, B or C or 1–5 are usually all that are required.

- If you feel like the reinforcement of a display, the backs of wardrobe doors are good places to tack up big sheets.

- Do use your chart or record as a dynamic instrument – let it point you to fresh tactics or encourage you to renewed efforts.

- Keep your records when your depression has lifted; they will be useful if you suffer a future relapse.

6. MOTIVATING YOURSELF

Motivation is crucially dependent on having goals to reach and being aware of the advantages of leaving the depressed state behind. So, the watchwords throughout are:

'I have something to aim for in the programme and it is of great value to me'

'When I think about how far I've come, I'm glad I took the first step and began the programme'

and

'If ever I feel like giving up or sense that my resolution is weak, I only have to glance at what I am now in comparison with what I was once, and I'm immediately empowered.'

4

The Betterment Programme

DEVELOPING A PERSONAL STRATEGY

This book contains many ideas for overcoming depression, some highly developed, others less so. Every one is of proven worth; almost all can be combined; none is essentially more useful than another. Because depression is an individual ailment no general prescriptions as to which idea or combination of ideas will best make up an individual programme are possible. What is provided here is a self-evaluation scheme so that you can judge your needs against a standardised, depression framework. You can then assess your existing particular strengths and weaknesses in terms of your own experience of depression. Such self-assessments will enable you to:

- establish a problem-priority

- find those strategies most relevant to your needs

- build an individual programme especially for you.

THE ACTION SITE FRAMEWORK

The framework comprises ten Action Sites, set out in detail in Chapter 5.

1. Waking thoughts and feelings
2. Routine depressive events
3. Other upsets
4. Relationships
5. Appetite
6. Upswings
7. Looking forward
8. Reinforcements
9. Unconscious mind
10. Sleeping and presleeping

SUMMARY OF ACTION SITES

1. Waking thoughts and feelings
In a developed depression the first thought on waking is usually a gloomy one and it's typically followed by a similar feeling. This mood, if once established, can persist throughout the day.

2. Routine depressive events
There is a range of semi-predictable events – radio news, morning mail, etc. – which may well contain demoralising or depressing items and which are best avoided, rescheduled or dealt with by techniques of thought-control.

3. Other upsets
Apart from routine depressants, there is always the chance that other thoughts or happenings may trigger down-moving moods, especially if these create exaggerated effects or are taken out of context.

4. Relationships
These can be vital factors in a depression – certain people can worsen moods, others can be supportive. Clear thinking and planning about relationships is essential.

5. Appetite
Food can play several roles in depression – as an escape or compensatory mechanism, as a method of self-punishment or as a useful mood- and morale-raiser. It is vital to be clear about food, and to develop ways of using it to enhance pleasure and build anticipation.

6. Upswings
All depressions involve variable upward shifts in mood, sometime occasional, often regular. They can be almost too small to notice or be bouts of intense excitement. But they can have their uses as opportunities to remotivate or take stock.

7. Looking forward
An almost defining condition of depression is an absence of forthcoming pleasurable events in your life. Organising these on a scheduled basis is an important factor in improvement.

8. Reinforcements
All actions taken to shift depression and all subsequent possible changes in mood need to be reinforced. So it is wise to prepare a store of reinforcements, e.g. pleasures and rewards.

9. Unconscious mind
One's unconscious mind is deeply implicated in a depression. Half-forgotten, parent-inspired guilt, urges that cannot find expression and memories that will not fade may all be unconscious factors in your depression.

10. Sleeping and presleeping
Poor sleeping and inadequate attitude-preparation for sleep are often features of depression. Presleeping programmes need to be organised to combat such problems.

USING THE ACTION SITE FRAMEWORK TO ORGANISE YOUR APPROACH

This framework not only organises the entire book, it also enables you to organise your own approach to using it. If you study the ten Action Sites in turn, you will soon form a working picture of how each is involved in your depression. Some may not seem very relevant, others you may never have considered, but others again will be suddenly familiar to you as a major part of your specific problems. Your task then is to assess each site on its merits as it is useful to you. Questions might include:

• Do I clearly understand the Action Site's purpose?

• Have I experienced any problems associated with the Action Site?

• Is it a major problem in my depression?

• Am I interested in what the Action Site might offer?

• What level of priority do I give to this Action Site?

This framework of Action Sites corresponds to the order of a typical depressive day. But all depressions are different and every day of a depression may reveal fresh emphasis, so there is no ideal order. Your task is to create your own order of relevance and priority. A useful method of combining both those features is to write a short note against each Action Site and then assign it a priority on a scale of 1–5.

A fully completed example of a framework with notes and prioritisations is supplied for you. In this example priorities for implementation are being assigned to Action Sites 1, 7 and 10. So, these will be our completer's priorities to start an attack on depression. Other sites have lower priorities and will be kept in reserve for tackling later. Our completer seems to have grasped the implications of all the sites despite the brevity of the descriptions. **If, however, you are uncertain at this point about any of the sites, and wish to explore them in much greater detail, you will find them in the next chapter**.

EXAMPLE OF COMPLETED FRAMEWORK

1. Waking thoughts and feelings
I do have these, and they do tend to run on through the day, so I welcome the chance to try to eliminate them at the start.

My priority for this site is (1)

2. Routine happenings
I'm pretty well wise to the kinds of happenings that can routinely depress me so I avoid or shunt them.

My priority for this site is (4)

3. Other upsets
I do get very easily discouraged and demoralised by events that I take personally and I tend to exaggerate happenings and lose a sense of proportion.

My priority for this site is (2)

4. Relationships
Most of my relationships are good and I aim to keep them that way.

My priority for this site is (5)

5. Appetite
I know that I could enjoy my food more so I'm getting into cooking and trying hard at some vegetable growing.

My priority for this site is (2)

6. Upswings
I hadn't noticed these rhythms before, but I realise now that they do occur and can be useful.

My priority for this site is (3)

7. Looking forward
I've just realised that I have absolutely nothing to look forward to, and no inclination to seek anything. This is serious and I must do something. But what?

My priority for this site is (1)

8. Reinforcements
I can see the need for building up a reserve of reinforcements so as to accentuate the positive in my life.

My priority for this site is (3)

9. Unconscious mind
I may be wrong but I don't recognise anyone or any thing that is having a depressing influence on me. So at the moment this is not a factor.

My priority for this site is (4)

10. Sleeping and presleeping
My sleeping is really bad. I'm usually up at least twice a night and can't get to sleep again because of fretting. I'm having nightmares too. I believe my sleeping is making my depression worse.

My priority for this site is (1)

EXERCISES

There are 29 important exercises in this book, spread across the ten Action Sites and several appendices. They provide the committed reader with:

- an opportunity in every case to gain mastery of the challenging psychological techniques that the Action Site poses

- a chance to build a selective programme of self-training, tailored and paced to individual requirements

- a continuous self-evaluation scheme based on progress.

There is great variety in the exercises. Most are simple, at least in form; they involve retraining routines or making detailed observations of intimate behaviour in order to bring about change in habit patterns. Most also require you to chart and record.

5

The Action Sites

ACTION SITE 1: WAKING THOUGHTS AND FEELINGS

The first thought on awakening is often crucial because it may chime with feelings and, if feelings and thinking are in sympathy, set a depressive pattern for the day. The surroundings of the waking thought have a fixing quality. They fix because, in the interval between full wakefulness and sleep there is little external stimulation, associations remain in the mind without being broken, critical awareness is absent and internal statements are untested. This uninterrupted nature of morning awakening is the decisive fixing factor, and so the decisive anti-depressive response is clear. It is to break established patterns by getting up and engaging in some distracting activity – not a routine task in which the depressive feeling can reassert itself, but something novel and uncharacteristic. You need to keep a stock of such activities to throw into this morning mechanism and interrupt it. A swim, a run, a telephone call, a dig of the garden plot, a sawing-up of something, a car repair, any task which is swift, easily arrangeable and sufficiently unconventional will do.

It is absolutely vital to get rid of the early-morning depressive mood. An awakening feeling can be deceptively comforting in its quiet certainty that everything will be a disaster throughout the day. Fail to break it up and the day *will* be a disaster, because events will be interpreted according to a depressive rule. There may be many depressive happenings during the day, but even if there are a few, or only one (and an unusual day contains nothing) each occurrence can be magnified out of all proportion.

Case history

Emma has her early mornings sussed
Emma remembered a catchy chorus from a review in her student days which ended,

> 'We know tomorrow
> Is bound to be hell!'

'They were right,' Emma said to herself, recalling the faces belting out the number, 'but only up to a point.' And the reason why she now doubted them somewhat was her morning drill. She had something for every morning. Each time she woke with that deadly feeling of gloom and certain knowledge that the mood would last the whole day, it was out of bed at once and choose an item. The range was wide: it included jogging (when the weather was good), a spot of hard cleaning, isometric exercises, yoga, a CD of the Time Bandits, coffee grinding, making phonecalls and many more. Some she could combine but whether she took them singly or in pairs, the purpose was the same – to smash the gloom utterly and jerk herself into at least a neutral state of mind. Only when she had satisfied herself that the waking mood had been suppressed by the item did she turn to breakfast.

And that was a creative event also. She believed in very tasty breakfasts. None of your cup-of-coffee-and-a-biscuit breakfasts for Emma. She went in for really delicious and sustaining little meals. Some of the best bacon in Europe bought by post from a farm shop at St Austell, eggs (she cooked them all ways) from her aunt's smallholding, bread and croissants baked from kits – Emma breakfasted on the best. And she gave herself plenty of time for the meal to settle before leaving for the train.

She knew that if she relaxed her pattern there was an even chance that the gloomy mood on waking could persist for the entire day, especially if some event occurred to reinforce it. So she was always alert for any fresh early morning item, whether gloom-shifting or breakfast-brightening, to build into her activities kit.

Points to note from Emma's drill

1. She reduces the time interval between waking up and getting up to a minimum.
2. She allows herself sufficient but not excessive time to work on the waking mood.
3. She has a kit of activities prepared which are appropriate to all possible circumstances.
4. She plans a confident early morning, with positive self-statements and pleasurable reinforcing activities.

Exercises

- The interval between waking up, getting up and getting started must be as short as possible. Put a wind-up timer by your bed and as soon as you wake, set it to a five minute bell. Try to reduce the interval before the pinger pings to the shortest possible period.

- The range of blocking and diverting activities must be wide and varied so as to allow as many alternatives as practicable. Start a systematic search-list exploring all possible categories of activity: domestic, sporting, exercise, education, entertainment, cooking, etc., and begin to build up sets of alternatives in each category.

- Prepare a kit of rejoinder phrases to counter depressive thoughts on immediate waking. Examples are, 'A new day is a gift', 'This could be my lucky day', 'A new day is now beginning', 'Every day is a new day', 'Yesterday is dead', etc. Rebut any depressive thought of feeling with a fresh chosen phrase.

- Start an early-morning diary and note your activities each day.

ACTION SITE 2: ROUTINE DEPRESSIVE EVENTS

A routine depressive event is one which will probably happen and when it does will darken an existing mood. Examples of such events might be the morning mail likely to bring news of rejection or failure or the newspaper carrying demoralising stories. Such depressants may mesh in a negative sense with an existing mood, particularly a vulnerable, early-morning one.

But a routine depressant is a *semi-predictable routine event*, in that its consequences are minimisable; not in the sense that rejections in the mail can be eliminated or news items brightened, but by adjusting the amount of impact to correspond with an up-swinging rather than a down-swinging mood or by avoiding the stimulus altogether. Leaving the house before the mail or paper arrives, arranging for them to be put aside unread until later and more complex techniques are all ways of disrupting the pattern of regular depressive risks and ensuring that eventual impacts are lessened.

Self-management tasks and skills required to tackle routine depressive events

Managing routine depressive events does require that the sufferer:

037780

- understands something of the connection between thoughts and feelings

- can make a timetable of likely depressive events either formally or informally

- is not deliberately *seeking* encounters with likely depressive events (this can occur with those who, for whatever reason, draw intimate satisfactions from their depressions)

- can use a variety of neutralising thought-control techniques for selective use.

Thoughts and feelings

What is the connection between thoughts and feelings? This is one of the great unasked, let alone answered, questions of psychology. But it is an essential question, nevertheless, in any book on coping with depression. We need some answers because of the possibility that, though feelings may not be under control to the extent that thoughts are, the power of the latter could offer a means whereby states of mood might be modified.

Traditional sayings suggest that control of thoughts is possible, at least in some circumstances. People assert that, 'they concentrated their minds', 'got a grip on the topic', 'thought the matter through' or 'dismissed the thought', all of which suggest a degree of conscious control.

On the other hand, feelings tend to 'wear off' or are 'lost' or undergo 'changes' or 'prey' upon the subject, indicating that they have a will of their own and do what they wish.

Evidence of feelings controlling or initiating thoughts is sparse but in the reverse direction we may note 'I got myself in the right frame of mind' and 'I thought better of it', both suggesting that moods may be altered.

Case history

Anne is systematically getting to grips with it
When Anne became depressed she determined to try to exert some element of rational control over her condition. This kind of self-management can often be helpful in producing improvement, but in depression, as she well knew, it is often difficult to find what it is that sets off the train of depressive thinking.

She knew she had to become skilful in the techniques of self-observation so that she could accurately detect what was causing her to be depressed. She searched for four kinds of trigger: those of physical circumstances, social settings, the behaviour of other people and her own thoughts.

One promising approach was to begin with the experience of the depressive thought and think through the history of her behaviour backwards in time before the thought or feeling began. She began to say to herself 'I thought that depressive thought and just before it I was in such and such a situation'. And she set herself to write down the events that occurred in the relatively short period of time, perhaps a few minutes or seconds, before she felt the depressive feeling intensify.

Before long she found that she was beginning to see a pattern in the triggers for the day's depression. To begin with there was getting up in the morning with a feeling of gloom which was always intensified by the early morning news. The news was generally bad or threatening and she noticed that within it there were elements that were particularly likely to trip off unpleasant thoughts. And then there was the noticeably depressing effect of the group of very attractive young women who got into the train with her at the station. Anne was forever comparing their chic clothes with her somewhat drab outfits. She noticed that at work she was frequently pushed into a deeper depression by people's tones of voice and attitudes – for example, the boss had a particularly sharp way of passing papers over to her for action and very often she noticed that his mouth was drawn up to one side as he did so. She had brooded about this and so she put it down as a possible trigger for depression. She made a written note too about the fact that before her lunch and even sometimes before the mid-morning coffee break, she felt particularly depressed for no adequate reason. She conjectured that this stimulus came from inside; possibly she was hungry and therefore her mood was lowered. After about a fortnight of making observations and notes of this kind, Anne was able to separate several kinds of triggers that seemed to produce undesirable feelings. There were various types but they usually boiled down to situations where she thought she was being disparaged or in some way compared unfavourably with others, where she was not sure what other people's evaluations of her really were, where she felt herself being threatened or when a group with whom she identified was threatened.

Several approaches now seemed open with three different triggers. She could, for example, avoid a trigger and reinforce herself for avoiding it, or she could avoid a trigger by substituting something else for it. Thus she could build in a pause between the trigger and its effect on her. Or she could attempt to relabel the trigger and make it seem more benevolent towards her and finally, of course, if it were a question of a chain of events leading finally to an increase in depression, then she could discover some means of breaking up the chain or scrambling it. For instance, when she got up in the morning she never now turned on the radio news; instead she put on a CD, a favourite one, of course. She took an earlier train rather than meet the girls who normally got into the same compartment as she did and, having taken an earlier train, she reinforced herself by regularly buying a magazine at the station bookstall. She labelled and relabelled events that occurred at work, including the apparently hurtful comments and gestures that the boss made. She introduced pauses too; for example, if the boss made any kind of remark that she would normally have interpreted as being derogatory or discouraging, she would pause before her reaction and say to herself, 'I must relabel this; I must relabel it in a way which sounds more cheerful and less critical'.

Then she exerted control over mealtimes. She brought forward her lunch-break by three quarters of an hour, thus enabling her to pick the best of the menu for the day. She also advanced her mid-morning coffee break by at least 20 minutes and ensured that she had something to eat as well. She discovered a chain of depression causing triggers in the evening which began with her arriving back at half-past five, doing some of the housework, washing up, cooking a meal, eating the meal and then finally at the end of the meal feeling depressed. So she broke that chain by cooking and eating the meal and then going on to complete the housework. Perhaps it was the planning, or perhaps the breaking up of old associations, but she noticed an improvement in her daily mood right from the start.

A self-management checklist for Anne's thinking

Anne will be even better able to regain control over her depressive thinking if she realises that:

- She may be *engaging in negative free-associations*, unconnected to an immediate stimulus, e.g. she may recall uncomfortable childhood rail journeys as she goes to work.

- She *can control her thinking*, especially those thoughts that seem to be automatic and are usually negative.

- She is *being selective* if she magnifies failure and minimises achievement.

- *Comparing herself unfavourably* with others is an excellent example of being selective – there are always others worse off than oneself.

- *Blaming herself* with no logical basis is irrational. Ideally, one takes responsibility *only for matters within one's control.*

- *Maintaining a range of 'shoulds' and 'musts'*, even when they are impracticable, is a common symptom of depression.

- *Jumping to conclusions* in a depression can be misleading and very easy to do.

- *Systematically devaluing* your past life and achievements is common in depressive thinking.

- *Polarising your thinking* – seeing everything as black or white – is also common in depression.

- *Projecting your negative thoughts* onto others, e.g. imagining they take the poor view of you that you take of yourself, is also a feature of depression.

Exercises

- Prepare your own thinking record chart from the points given above.

- Study carefully Action Sites 3 and 8, noting the range of techniques for thought-analysis and control they describe.

- Keep a daily record for three months of thoughts, actions and outcomes.

ACTION SITE 3: OTHER UPSETS

By no means all events with depressive meanings or consequences happen on a routine or semi-predictable basis. Often they occur out of the blue, seemingly accidentally. For example, a depressive can often be overwhelmed by a burst of self-critical or derogatory thoughts, which were triggered by nothing in particular, but are very persistent and difficult to shift. Thoughts of this type have an especially bitter quality and are usually accompanied by sharply melancholic feelings. Examples are 'I'm useless, always have been and always will be', or 'Why do I always seem to fail? It's because I'm no good.'

Thoughts of this kind, if they are allowed to run on unchecked, can brew up deeply despondent moods. It's vital to learn techniques to stop them developing. There are such techniques available, as we shall demonstrate in this case history.

Case history

John is perfecting thought-stopping
Constantly brooding about his inadequacies, and the fact that he had failed, was doing John no good at all. Such thoughts were filling up all his thinking, blocking him from really constructive planning, and giving him the absorbed look of a man who was weighed down by the pressures of the world. John determined to try and control his thoughts by using techniques of thought-control. He asked a friend to act as counsellor and prepared the following plan.

First he drew up a list of self-destructive inner statements that he was apt to use about himself. Then he and the friend sat quietly together and John concentrated on the first and most frequent on the list. When it was running clearly through his mind he signalled to the friend who said loudly '*STOP*'. John repeated it, with his friend coming in decisively with '*STOP*'. Then he picked a second thought from the list, concentrated upon it, and, without signalling, stopped himself. Another thought followed which was signalled and then stopped by his friend and so on. They had several sessions of this stopping until John was capable of switching off any thought by himself. Next, John developed a method of emphasising positive thoughts. He drew up a short list of twelve positive statements like 'Things cannot get any worse . . . they are going to get better', and then he thought of pleasurable scenes to imagine, like visualising himself on a secluded beach with drinks and entertainment to hand. He practised bringing these scenes into his mind with speed and clarity. Next, he and his friend practised the reinforcement, John repeating to himself the positive statement and telling his friend that it was clear in his mind. His friend then said clearly 'reinforcement' whereupon John switched to imagining the pleasurable scene he had practised. They repeated and repeated this procedure with different phrases until John could switch to the scene without any verbal reinforcement.

Finally, John did not need his friend to be with him to manage the switch. As soon as anything like a self-destructive or self-blaming thought came into his head it was blocked by a pleasurable scene before it had a chance to establish itself.

Controlling over-reactions

Thought-stopping is a very useful tool for dealing with obtrusive thoughts. But such thoughts are only one of a series of challenges faced in a depression. Another very serious type is inappropriate reaction. There are two prominent examples, catastrophising and personalising.

Catastrophising

What is catastrophising? It is a proneness to exaggerate events and their impact on the self so as to justify extreme emotional reactions such as terror, despair and shock. Catastrophising is a particular feature of established depression. The sense of proportion that usually controls judgement of events and their personal significance is badly distorted and the catastrophiser experiences abnormal emotional responses that are clearly unjustified by the particular happenings.

Although some catastrophisers have a long history of exaggerated responses, predating their depressions, almost all have some insight into the condition. They can recognise but not necessarily regulate the process, which seems to involve a predetermined exaggerated response to a stimulus with no time for consideration or modification. The way to gain control over catastrophising, an essential link in the chain of a depression, is via the gap which naturally exists between stimulus and response, or an event and the emotions that follow.

Gaining control over catastrophising

First, it is essential to build up a record of the frequency of catastrophising and the particular type of events that cause it to occur. Charting for frequency is not difficult; a simple weekly record is quite sufficient. Establishing types may be more difficult, but the simple notation:

a = events that involve other people and their unpredictability
b = events that involve machines or systems
c = intimate events – health problems, etc.
d = external events – the national and international news, etc.
e = money upsets

is a start. Two months of charting should provide a good record of when and how the incidents occur. By that time a considerable degree of control sensitivity should be establishing itself as follows: 'I can recognise the type of event that usually causes me to react in an exaggerated manner.'

'I know there is a moment, not much more, when I have the power to decide how I will react.'

'I know that this opportunity will slip away if I do not take it.'

'I realise I have a wider range of ways to react than I once thought.'

'I can choose the way I will react and my choice will depend not on how I reacted in the past, but on my judgement in the present.'

'However I react it will not be on the basis of my previous catastrophising habit.'

'I can react in any way I wish.'

Personalising

Personalising is a particularly depression-inducing proneness for making the self the focus of meaning of events. All happenings have some self-reference, of course; the very fact of their being perceived or remembered guarantees this. But personalising goes much further; its self-reference in terms, say, of impact on self-esteem, prospects, reputations, etc., becomes a constant habit of mind and therefore events are forever challenging mood and morale.

We vitally need to keep ourselves free of personalising by systematically checking and modifying any and every instance when we find ourselves connecting emotionally with events that are essentially not about us.

Checklist for reducing personalising

- A very common type of personalising is the idea of reference, usually experienced as the ultra self-conscious statement, 'They are all looking at me'. A good counter-statement is

'How much notice do *I* take of someone leaving his seat in a cinema, or ordering drinks at a bar or doing anything that momentarily seems to give them an audience? So, all I have to do is to behave casually, and just like me, nobody will pay the slightest attention.'

- Less common is personalising of events, e.g. deep upset because a team has lost; grief because a bid has failed; embarrassment and shame for a celebrity humiliated. For these we need test questions. 'How much has it affected me materially in the past in terms of loss of love, income or support?' If the answer is 'Not much', then the next question is, 'So just what is this feeling about?', then the conclusion is plain, 'I am interested but not personally upset'.

We can go a little further and, if necessary, try some paradoxical techniques. Unvoiced statements such as, 'If they look at me they may learn something', or even the slightly arrogant, 'I'm not surprised they're staring, I'm worth staring at', can be effective if for no other reason than that they give a humorous boost to morale in a situation when being downcast is the norm.

Case history

Paul is attempting to get a grip on thoughts and reactions
'There is a routine for emotional response control', Paul said to himself, 'and I'd better run through it to make sure I have it right. There are three stages. The first is the ability to sense in advance what my reactions are likely to be to any important event. The second is the skill of being able to suspend any immediate response until I have had time to consider what should be appropriate. And the third is to make the right response, the one which is both rational and emotionally economic. I have to remember that 'event' is a shorthand term for a whole range of happenings which could include things said and done, experiences of every kind and deliberate or involuntary thoughts. Event is anything I could react to; the significant thing that sets me off. Or rather did set me off, because my aim is to stop being a passive, automatically-reacting personality and become empowered.

'Establishing the routine is the simple part; putting it into practice will be demanding. I'm carrying much past baggage in the shape of the styles of emotional reaction I've been taught or taught myself. I was prone to what is called 'catastrophising', that is exaggerating the significance of a happening in my response. Another of my styles was 'black or white judgements'; there were no shades of grey, no middle paths I could glimpse to give me the chance of taking my time or judging a situation. I was also quite unable to label things correctly or reassign them less threatening meanings, and so was constantly risking overreactions.

'But with effort and luck this old performance will change. The essential factor is my skill at creating a pause in the 'stimulus to response' process, sufficient to give me time to consider. I must always keep in mind that I have a choice. Typically this will not be *how* to react, though occasionally I will be able to choose between emotions. It's more likely to be the degree of reaction, or no reaction at all, that I can decide on, if I can create and extend that crucial pause. I'm going to become more and more skilful with practice because even the smallest success in this area breeds success, and also because of the reinforcement from others which will come when they see I am getting a grip on thoughts and reactions at long last.'

In order to firm up his resolve, Paul drew the two thoughts and reactions diagrams. The first depicted his automatic state where A (the event or thought) led instantly to B (the response or result). But the second introduced a middle element, S for self, so that the

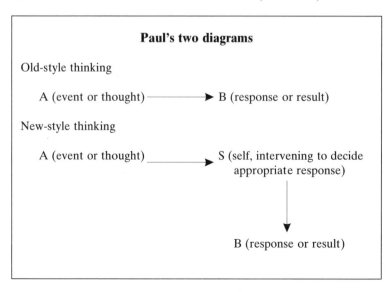

Paul's two diagrams

Old-style thinking

A (event or thought) ⟶ B (response or result)

New-style thinking

A (event or thought) ⟶ S (self, intervening to decide appropriate response)

↓

B (response or result)

diagram showed A (event or thought) then S (self-decider) and B (response or result).

Guilt

In depression, guilt – real, imaginary or possessing some inter-mediate and difficult to establish basis in fact – can create a fearful torment. Whether depression generates such guilt or vice versa is still unclear; a bit of both is probably nearest the truth.

Whether it is a symptom or origin, however, out of control guilt is a most unwelcome feature of a depression and one which all sufferers would be glad to rid themselves of. As regards Action Sites, it straddles both routine depressants and other upsets. It can routinely recur, or occasionally and painfully make itself felt. The balance of probability lies with the latter, which is why it is placed at this point.

Notes on guilt

- Feelings of guilt can intensify during a depression, a fact that offers you opportunities. If you can recall that the feeling of guilt which seems so sharp now was at one time hardly given a passing thought, then something of the grip of guilt may be loosened.

- It hardly needs mention that the guilt a sufferer from depression feels is *hugely disproportionate* to the acts and consequences that originally caused it.

- Intrusive guilty thoughts can be eradicated through the thought stopping techniques of this Action Site.

- Guilt can be eased by constructive, well-judged restitution or apology.

- Guilt can also be markedly blunted by carefully planned and sincerely undertaken leisure counselling (see appendix on leisure counselling). This should follow the confrontation, sub-stitution model, and take the form of some hobby, activity or interest that directly opposes the spirit or story of the guilt. Take, for example, the case-history of a man who has spent his youth and early manhood shooting birds. In middle-age he is eaten up with guilt which he decisively eases by joining the RSPB, becoming a local committee member and building up a thriving bird sanctuary near his home.

Self-esteem

Many of the problems arising in this Action Site have the effect of undermining self-esteem. Three types of recovery from loss of self-esteem are described and analysed in the appendices.

Exercises

- Referring to the case history of John, perfect the two thought-stopping techniques with a friend's help, and then record weekly for three months your success in suppressing or diverting intrusions.

- Set up a chart recording the weekly frequency of your 'catastrophising' and its types. Then, using Paul's new-style thinking technique, try a three month trial of the technique.

- Set up a chart recording the weekly frequency of your 'personalising'. Again, using Paul's new-style thinking and the rejoinder techniques suggested, try a three month trial of the technique.

ACTION SITE 4: RELATIONSHIPS

There is no doubt that ways of relating to other people are important in depression. Two particularly significant aspects stand out – reinforcement given to your depression when others see the state, and methods by which you use others as tools to intensify your depressive mood. To some extent, varying between individuals, an obviously depressed person attracts remarks and acts that tend to intensify the depression. This is true when you are not deliberately posing as a depressive, deliberately exaggerating your mood or blocking your chances, but more particularly when you are. Depressions are not states of isolation, though they do require a measure of detachment to flourish. Because they are not detached but connected with other people, they become little dramas with you playing the tragic role. As with dreams and fantasies there are strong satisfactions to be gained from such role-playing with you enjoying the attention the role promotes, the criticisms attracted, or the encouragement received. All parts of the personality – the guilt-ridden, punishment-seeking, love-needing and drama-desiring – may gain in their different ways.

Targeting inappropriate personal myths

Some depressives have personal myths (many of which are detailed in the following list) which are tenaciously clung to but often cause suffering when they clash inappropriately with circumstances.

Potentially inappropriate personal myths

- **The Hero:** do you visualise yourself as a hero or heroine, dramatically beset by enemies/difficulties, but holding your own?

- **The Victim:** do you visualise yourself as a victim continuously surrounded by forces or people stronger than yourself?

- **The Saviour:** do you visualise yourself as a saviour; not so much a miracle-worker, but a steady solver of problems and upholder of weaker sisters and brothers?

- **The Scapegoat:** do you visualise yourself as a blame-taker; as somebody who is singled out for criticism?

- **The Disciple:** do you visualise yourself as willingly dominated by either an ideology or person?

- **The Rogue:** do you visualise yourself as not sharing the moral values of those around; and ready to exploit them?

- **The Joker:** do you visualise yourself as wholly committed to raising a laugh; using humour as a weapon?

- **The Guru:** do you visualise yourself as the wise sage of the establishment?

- **The Retainer:** do you visualise yourself as a traditional, time-honoured, super-reliable subordinate, with occasional inverted powers?

- **The Sceptic:** do you visualise yourself as having reasonable doubt concerning the aims, quality or calibre of others and their work?

None of these personal myths is necessarily irrational if set in the appropriate context, and played with restraint. There are situations in which heroes or heroines are necessary and the group/institution/society applauds their successful role-taking. Problems arise, however, when the context is not so appropriate or when confusions between different roles take place. For example:

- A persistent Hero is snubbed by the lack of a crisis.
- There are too many Jokers for the group to tolerate.
- A Saviour decides to discard one or more of his/her Retainers or Disciples.
- A Retainer tries to play Sceptic when all things point to fundamentalism.
- A Victim decides not to be a victim.
- A Guru is outsmarted by a new/younger Guru.
- A Retainer discovers that whatever counts, it's not loyalty.

What we see here is a series of role-changes/abandonments or inappropriate part-matchings, which can cause great distress if they are challenged by circumstances.

Peter, the subject of our next case history, is a fine example of a repudiated Guru or Saviour, with all the bitterness this entails, and the depressive, self-torturing, moods it creates.

Case history

Peter, whose myth has failed
Peter waxed quite indignant when the deputy head suggested he might be 'burned-out'. 'I'm not bloody well burned-out,' he said. 'That's a fancy American term for bored professionals. I'm not bored, I'm depressed and for pretty good reasons too.' The deputy head fluttered off, sympathising unconvincingly.

'Pity he went,' said Peter, 'because I was going on to tell him why; as if he cared. He's part of the problem.'

Peter's staff-room audience now began to excuse itself and sidle out. But Peter had hit his stride and was not to be deterred by fewer and fewer listeners.

'I was going to ask him to put himself in my position,' he went on. 'Fifty-one, married and still a sizeable chunk of the mortgage to pay off. Consistently passed over for promotion and having fruitlessly attended 26 short-lists. And going bald and discovering himself increasingly impotent in every sense.'

This touch of the intimate acted as a holding factor on Peter's diminishing audience.

'Does he wake every morning with a feeling of despair?' he demanded. 'Does he reflect then that there's precious little chance of amounting to much? Is he sitting on the memory of a couple of text-books written, but then rejected by at least a dozen educational publishers, to say nothing of a novel? No, of course he bloody hasn't. That's why he's a member of the management echelon at the age of thirty-five.'

'I'm not surprised that a man with your capacity for bitter eloquence is dissatisfied,' said Eric, one of Peter's younger and more thoughtful colleagues.

'Yes, well I am supposed to be an English expert,' Peter said. 'And there is a whacking gap between my ambition and my realisation. And you'll recall that Nietzsche said that unless you carry chaos within you, you'll never give birth to a dancing star. I've got the chaos right enough, but where's the dancing star?'

'What do you expect from teaching?' Eric asked him.

'I can't recall what I expected,' Peter said. 'Just as I couldn't describe in this half-baked and melancholy state exactly where the interest went. Results, conceivably, but the results are impossible to assess. Feedback, but all one gets is blow-backs.'

'I know the cure for you,' said Eric brightly, 'a change of job.'

'Pray, do me a favour,' Peter said. 'Who do you think is going to employ a man whose only skill is stopping kids moving their lips while they read?'

Depressives like Peter are in real trouble

Though their actual depressions could be termed chronic and moderate rather than sudden and severe, sufferers like Peter with very deeply disrupted life-scripts face real trouble. Theirs is a malady of the spirit as much as anything else, and they are almost certain to have lost, and to be losing, significant amounts of self-esteem.

Self-esteem is not simple to repair; luck and redirection may help but the more likely outcome is a holding operation designed to prevent the depression intensifying.

There are three types of self-esteem loss: transient, chronic and severe. Peter falls into the third category where, appropriate to the problem's severity, the focus is very detailed.

Systematically improving crucial relationships

Fortunately not every depressive is in the kind of relationships *cul-de-sac* that has Peter trapped. Most have room to manoeuvre, perhaps even to make a turn. To manage this successfully, however, they will certainly need to carry out an audit of depression-significant relationships, looking at each with a view to assessing its importance and the degree to which it can be improved or neutralised. Our next case history demonstrates such an audit in moderately successful action.

Case history

Patrick takes stock of his relationships

'I know I'm not fond of myself,' Patrick said, silently 'and that means or is said to mean that my relationships with others are always likely to be frail, complicated, distant or fleeting. But I'm reluctant to accept this situation as unalterable, especially as I'm now deeply into self-understanding and management. So, I'm going to take stock of my existing and, to an extent, past relationships with the aim of discovering what part each plays in my depression and, as I put that behind me, how each can help or hinder. I'll look at four key relationships in turn: my partner Amanda, my mother Agnes, my colleague Tony and my friend John.

'One very important factor in my depression, or at least the view I took of myself, was the educational gap between Amanda and myself, to my disadvantage. Amanda has a degree in Arts from Sussex, but I left school at 18 with three A levels. However, as part of my leisure-counselling programme, I enrolled for an engineering degree at the Open University. This is no easy option but I'm in my very succcessful second year, and in twelve months time I shall be lining up to receive my degree from Lord Melvyn Bragg or whomever. And then, if not before, I shall finally feel Amanda's equal. But, in fact, my confidence has been growing with each project or essay for which I earn B++ or above and, as of now, I can almost feel freed of my inferiority baggage.

'My mother Agnes is a problem of a different kind. It isn't just her living in sheltered accommodation that has depressed me; I've come to terms with that and the guilt it has caused. No, the most depression-making part of visiting my mother, which I do each week, is the childhood memories aroused. Mine was a mother from hell, endlessly criticising and ridiculing me by comparison with her nephews and absolutely incapable of demonstrating a shred of real affection. But I have learned techniques of re-labelling, thought-stopping and minimising which I apply each time my mother's reality eats into my confidence and attempts to set my memories running.

'My colleague Tony presents me with another kind of challenge. Although we've never discussed it, we both know that when the present contract runs out in two years' time, there will be work for one and that one will not be me. I realise that I'm ducking a challenge but more realistically the challenge is not equal; Tony is more experienced and his wife is the Principal's cousin. So it is almost inevitable that if I stay, in due course I shall have to go. To be pushed out would be a blow to my self-esteem I could not risk and, therefore, I shall have to start looking for a new job very soon. Not that this will be easy in terms of timing, to say nothing of my poor interview technique. But there is no alternative.

'There are also few alternatives on offer in regard to my relationship with my friend John. To put it bluntly I need him badly as a confidant and support, and have relied upon him since childhood as my intimate friend. Unfortunately he has recently married and his wife has taken a dislike to Amanda and me. She has more or less cut him off from us, a wounding development since he used to come to stay regularly before his marriage.

'If I'm to rebuild my friendship with John, I will have to meet him by myself on neutral ground. In the past we used to do this occasionally through London theatre and cinema trips. I don't imagine remaking these arrangements will be easy, but I'm too old to expect new friendships.'

Formalising the social audit
Patrick's approach to his varied relationship problems is neces-sarily informal. But to ensure that we provide a comprehensive guide to social auditing, we need to set out a simple framework which will cover the widest range of individual requirements.

Framework for an audit
1. State the name of the person for audit.
2. State the relationship to the auditor.
3. State relationship category: family, friend, acquaintance, colleague, etc.
4. Describe the significance of this person for your depression.
5. State the duration of this influence.

6. State steps taken to modify the influence.
7. State success or otherwise of such steps.
8. Describe fresh strategies.
9. Note success or otherwise of fresh strategies.

Exercises

- Confront the issue of loneliness as an important factor in depression by studying the case history of Melissa in the appendix on leisure counselling. Develop your own leisure-counselling plan along the lines suggested.

- If necessary, write your own relationships audit and set up appropriate programmes to help the situations.

- Study the list of personal myths and describe any instance known to you when clashes between myth and reality led to depression.

- Consult the appendix on self-esteem and carry out the repair or sustaining regimes described, as appropriate.

ACTION SITE 5: APPETITE

This site is concerned with food and eating which, with sex, forms one of the two key appetites of our lives. Both are vital pleasure-resources in the fight against depression. Both are under remorseless attack from a range of different directions. But both can be salvaged as important aids to happier living if their full contributions are grasped and obstacles to enjoyment are assessed and eliminated.

Six destructive slogans

'I have no appetite.'
    'If I eat too much I'll gain weight.'
    'If I don't eat I'll punish myself by becoming thin and reward myself by winning other people's pity and concern.'
    'I'm so overweight already. I must stop eating.'
    'I must eat.'
    'I have no desire to eat anything. To eat is to become involved, and I don't intend to become involved.'
    These are all self-statements linking to various depressive attitudes.

This site provides a range of different self-management approaches. For Action Site 7, Looking forward, organising expectancy in terms of food is not difficult. An enormous variety of new or exotic foods is available for those who can afford to eat out. Growing your own food, if you have access to a garden or even a window-box, is an excellent way of building up anticipations. The time spans from planting to eating can be short or long according to choice or season. Appetisers, vitamins and tonics, in moderation, are also useful if you find they work for you.

Some of the techniques designed to break up sequences of depressive thoughts – the exercises in Action Site 1, for example – can be surprisingly appetite-creating. You may associate eating with the depression-inducing circumstances of noise, rush, penalties, threats, arguments, competitiveness, nausea, dirt and smells and not the appetising smells of cooking or the delights of good company. These unwanted intrusions need to be ruthlessly kept out and better features brought in. Tablecloths, for example, ease the eyes, symbolise freshness and provide a breathing space in the day.

Case history

Ursula is rebalancing her eating
There was no doubt about it, Ursula had let herself drift into some bad food habits. She was finding no satisfaction in her eating at all; slumped in front of the television, picking at a boil-in-the-bag, she would often feel full after a couple of mouthfuls and more often than not be attacked by a real bout of indigestion within an hour of finishing her so-called meal.

Intuitively, she knew that food and everything that surrounds it is one of the two key intimate factors in keeping up personal morale, the other being sex. 'My sex life is totally shot at the moment,' Ursula said to herself, 'so I'd better concentrate on the food.'

Ursula decided to tackle the problem from two directions: planning and preparing, and eating and enjoying.

For the first she created a weekly menu plan which allowed for a shift forward one day each month. The plan organised breakfast and supper but left each actual meal free for variation. For example, cereal breakfasts on Saturdays and Sundays permitted a choice between four possible items, while fish supper on Tuesdays opened the options to all the fishmonger had to offer.

At the same time Ursula concentrated on cooking, specialising on baking and marinading and introducing the widest range of herbs and spices. Although her menu rota was fixed, she always took the opportunity to invite a friend for supper if she felt the meal would suit. This gave a big boost to her own enjoyment and anticipation, both very important to the self-management she was struggling to achieve.

And she concentrated too on the act of eating, realising that in order to gain the emotional benefits she would have to:

- Focus on the exciting flavours of a dish, mixing the varied items creatively so as to give her tastebuds full satisfaction.

- Take each meal slowly and chew every mouthful thoroughly, thus giving her appetite time to adjust itself.

- Establish a good sitting posture for eating, thus avoiding wind and indigestion.

Via her eating programme Ursula discovered the true meaning of the phrase 'cooking with love and eating with contentment'. In terms of anticipation and realisation, food had become the vital counter-depressive interest in her life. But there was still something more that she could do. Ursula had no garden; she lived in a tower block flat but there was a balcony, and it faced south-west. So she began a little vegetable garden. It was nothing ambitious – salads in trays, tomatoes in grow-bags and some Chinese beans in a box in the corner. But it was a new interest, and gave her a feeling of fresh empowerment. More than anything else, there was something to look forward to, in summertime at least.

Exercises

There are four useful areas for rebalancing food pleasure:

- meal planning
- sociable eating
- concentrating on eating itself
- growing one's own food.

Study the four in the light of the information in the site. Then pick two for priority action, devising programmes for each on the basis of stated objectives, routes to attainment and records of achievement. When you are satisfied with your progress, work with the remaining two in the same fashion.

ACTION SITE 6: UPSWINGS

Upswings – the rising phases of depression in which periods of optimism reign – can, if recognised, be most valuable tactical periods in the struggle for control. In an upswing (and each day of depression may yield one) anticipated activities can be arranged, and plans made which may not be possible at other times because of lack of energy. Relationships can be re-established or warmed if they have cooled during the downswing periods, and credit in emotional social terms built up for periods when you might be relatively inaccessible, or seem cold, remote or preoccupied. Achievement can also be aimed for with an increasing sense of personal efficiency. In upswings, thinking is frequently speeded, word and phrase-fluency eased, bodily posture freed – all elements creating behaviour which can build up substantial credit balances.

Why upswings are important
Upswings are opportunities for various kinds of remedial action in tackling depression. By far the most important role they can play is actually *beginning such action and overcoming the starting inertia that often inhibits a depressive from making the first move.*

Also important is the leverage an upswing can give to the planning of future events. During an upswing pleasures can be scheduled which transform your here-and-now into anticipation, thus creating fantasies and all manner of compensatory and reassuring ideas.

Thirdly, an upswing has intrinsic value. Its very appearance, sometimes without warning, is a warrant of better things possible. Most significantly, it can be a tactical asset in its own right. By studying it, the sufferer may induce it to become more regular, extend its periods and, perhaps, even intensify the upward trend.

Case history

Kevin makes the most of upswings
Kevin had been told that as soon as you recognised an upswing you needed to ask yourself some questions and make some resolutions. The questions were:

- When did it start?

- What triggered it?

Only approximate answers might be possible.
And the resolutions were to:

- make use of it

- try to extend it

- try to make it recur.

As far as he could judge, Kevin's upswing had begun in the early afternoon; just after a particularly good lunch and significantly before the three o'clock rush started. What had triggered it was a mystery but that pretty woman from Accounts could have been responsible with her, 'That's a nice tie, Kevin'.

Whatever it was, his mood, which had been especially low in the morning, had lifted and he felt more or less normal, even very mildly cheerful. How could he use this upswing, try to extend it and make it recur?

Kevin knew that the three o'clock frenzy could only be managed without stress and aftershocks if everything ran ultra-smoothly. That required preparation, so he set up all the software meticulously, checking the time allowances and giving himself plenty of fall-back. He had never been so ready in his entire career as, sure enough, three o'clock struck and the whole office began to jump. It was just after four when he eventually surfaced but the hour had run smoother than ever before, better than he could have hoped.

Just after half-past four, with his mood still cheerful, he decided to try some reinforcement by ringing Mel.

'What's that I'm hearing about a rave on Saturday week?' he asked. 'Twenty quid a ticket; I've got three left,' replied Mel.

So Kevin had something pleasurable to anticipate and ten days in which to do the anticipating which definitely reinforced the upswing, and made it possible that each time he thought about pleasures to come, there would be pressure on his prevailing mood to move upwards. But what about the upswing's actual trigger? That pretty woman from Accounts might be prompted to say 'That's another nice tie Kevin,' provided, of course, he laid in a stock of interesting ties and discovered precisely when she broke for lunch so as to 'accidentally' bump into her at the serving counter.

Kevin logged the answers to the two questions on his progress chart, and kept the three resolutions in his mind.

Exercises
Prepare a chart which will record:

- dates and times of your upswings

- notes of possible triggerings.

Make entries for a period of at least six months on this chart.
Prepare a resolutions chart showing:

- what use you made of each upswing

- how you endeavoured to extend it

- what steps you took to try to make it recur.

ACTION SITE 7: LOOKING FORWARD

Depressives look back to the past. The past, in essence, seems to dominate them. The present is indeed the depression but the influence of the future is negligible, except insofar as the future is deemed to be full of foreboding. *Optimistic anticipations*, however, are a vital key to neutralising a depression. They require the organising or planning of future pleasurable events which can be savoured and contrasted with the black realities of the present. Such anticipations can vary: a walk, holiday, visit, new car, new suit, theatre or concert ticket. They will be different, of course, requiring varying degrees of commitment, money and planning. But they are all part of a positive future and thus contributors to a bearable present.

Taking precautions

Deliberately looking forward to a pleasure always carries with it the risk that the pleasure will not meet final expectations. It is unrealistic to expect perfection, and sensible to seek ways of ensuring that the failure of an anticipated pleasure to deliver fully does not ruin the value of the event as a mood-sustainer. Useful precautionary points to note are:

- Don't put all your emotional eggs in one basket but spread the anticipated pleasure over a chain of future events.

- Precondition yourself to enjoy specifically reliable aspects of the pleasure in store (see planning paper note).

- Arrange for the pleasure to be shared with a friend, thus guaranteeing social satisfaction at least.

- Deliberately rehearse your reaction to the possibility of cancellation, etc. For example, prepare yourself by thinking, 'What else can I do if . . . ?'

Case history

Len is looking forward to the match, but keeping his fingers crossed

Len had been really lucky. He'd drawn three away fixtures in the club coach lottery, so that was something to look forward to for the entire season. They were well-spaced; the first was in a fortnight.

All teams seemed to rise to the occasion when they played City away. But most did not rise quite enough and so Len was braced for a disappointment. Not that Town had been playing badly, quite the reverse; it was third from the top of the division. But City was City.

Len would be sitting next to Colin on the coach. Colin was always good for a laugh; invariably cheerful, though heaven knows what he had to be cheerful about with that leg of his. Len always enjoyed the City trip. The road went over the Trent at Gunthorpe, and he had many happy boyhood memories of fishing there with his father.

Len had been on an away to Bolton when the coach had broken down 20 miles from their destination. They never saw that match. But this away they would see, regardless, Len promised himself. 'If we break down or can't get in the ground,' Len said to himself, 'we find a pub, and settle down to watch it there.'

Activity scheduling

Activity scheduling can be formally planned in clusters of six activities, each cluster to extend over a period of about four weeks. This gives ample time for planning arrangements, allowing ideas to arise and, most important, anticipatory conditioning – the savouring of the event in advance. It doesn't mean that the schedule needs be absolutely rigid in a timing sense but you should practise the conditioning at the appropriate time. Don't forget that the third aspect of the activity at the end of every planning paper carries a double message, a pleasant preview of a future happening, *plus a signal that the next set of scheduled activities must now be planned.*

Activity Schedule Sheet

Planning Paper – Six Activities

    Activity scheduled (state activity in simple words)

    Date scheduled

    First aspect of activity (state aspect)

    I am bound to enjoy . . . .

    Second aspect of activity (state aspect)

    I am bound to enjoy . . . .

   *Third aspect of activity (state aspect)

    I am bound to enjoy . . . .

---

   * If this is the final activity, I must plan another cluster now.

Food and sex as basic pleasures

In terms of anticipation potential these basic drives have the power to transform depressive moods. Mental rehearsals of their forthcoming pleasures can form key elements in formal and informal activity scheduling. In order to be effective, however, they must have some if not most pleasure-enhancing necessities: surprise, variety, creativity, spontaneity and ingenuity.

Developing hobbies, activities and interests for anticipation purposes

Systematised looking forward will clearly require either a wide range of hobbies, activities and interests or the skill and technique to elaborate, and ring the changes on a selected few. Leisure counselling provides the necessary discovery, renewal and developmental skills to generate anticipation materials, and readers are advised to study the extensive appendix at the end of the book for guidance. The Pleasure-relaxation appendix is also very relevant.

Exercises

- Study the case history of Len, and informally anticipate a hobby, activity or interest, making use of the subject's precautions. Assess the pleasure gained.

- Set up a series of activity schedules, say three, covering twelve weeks. Prepare a schedule sheet for the first six activities. Assess the results at the end of a full series.

- Study Action Site 5 for appropriate anticipatory materials.

- Study the Leisure counselling appendix for guidance on developing or extending interests.

ACTION SITE 8: REINFORCEMENTS

The term reinforcement refers to all those possible ways to emphasise the positive in yourself and others, and thereby reduce negative, depressive and defeatist experiences. We can reinforce ourselves and others by a series of *well-chosen thoughts and acts*, all of which give pleasure and are designed to produce a repetition of what has pleased and reassured us and others.

Reinforcement applied

If reinforcement is to be effective, it has to follow rapidly what we desire to re-experience. This requires our reinforcement to be at the ready, in stock, maintained or planned for whatever mode is appropriate because unless it is closely linked, it will not reinforce.

Reinforcing acts

These are specially directed to rewarding or promoting positive behaviour either in oneself or others and by such means reshaping a lifestyle away from a depressive trend. This reinforcement requires a strong and consistent self-change attitude and a degree of well-planned creativity. It also needs timing, luck and judgement and elements of practice, as shown in the following case history.

Case history

Jacky discovers action reinforcements

There was something almost, but not quite, accidental about the way Jacky discovered reinforcements. She was listening to Radio 2 one morning when a bouncy American voice, which sounded very old-fashioned, began to sing.

Though it was a very old song, it was sung with such gusto and had a wonderful catchy tune so Jacky decided to ask her mother if she remembered the full words from her childhood. When asked, her mother smiled and sang, tapping her feet.

'Accentuate the positive
Eliminate the negative
Latch on to the affirmative
Don't mess with Mr In-between.'

And so Jacky had the full first verse which was all she wanted. It was quite magical how this jumpy old ditty, popular when her mother was five years old, summed up all she needed to know about becoming and staying positive. And positive was what she needed to be if she were to shake off her depressive moods.

She started as she meant to go on at the bus stop. The driver was his usual dour self, but Jacky gave him a glorious smile as she offered her 95p and, marvels never ceasing, he smiled back at her.

When she was at work, they had one of the longest unbroken

sequences ever experienced. 'This deserves a celebration,' Jacky announced, bringing out a box of Belgian chocolates from her desk and handing them round the section. And then almost immediately they had a breakdown. 'Don't brood on it,' Jacky told herself as she rang for services to fix it. 'Just take yourself off for your coffee-break and perhaps it will be up and running when you come back.'

Sure enough, services *had* fixed it, for once, when she got back, and then they had a clear run to lunch. For lunch Jacky had a predatory venture planned. She would drift into the Otter and if, by chance, that dishy chap from the other branch was there, she would just stroll over to his table and join him. The word was that his partner had walked out on him. He might be quite a prospect for a single, lustful, girl.

And it turned out just as planned, though she made one or two precautionary mental arrangements just in case. He *was* at the Otter (her timing was precise) and she sauntered over, jacketless, to join him. And he was eating pâté. 'I do a brilliant salmon and anchovy mousse,' she said at exactly the right point in her presentation.

As they walked back into the main building he asked if she were booked on the theatre trip. She confessed she wasn't, but ten minutes and two internal calls later, she was, calculating that £50 for theatre, dinner and coach was very reasonable and would give her an excellent chance of sitting with him.

Her good mood even survived the three o'clock messenger with an absolutely horrendous task for her. Jacky grabbed it from him, gave him the sweetest smile, glanced at the first ten words and shoved it smartly under her pile. 'Just let it mature a while,' she said, out loud, grinning like a dolphin.

Perhaps as a counter-stroke to that piece of elimination, she suddenly had an idea. They certainly needed reinforcement in Warranty, so she sent them a reassuring note. 'Don't worry about overload,' said her message, 'just pass them along to me; we've spare capacity at present.'

'Stop worrying about your mother's mood when you get back tonight,' she prompted herself, when later on at the end of the afternoon she began to think about the evening ahead. 'All you have to do is to call in that new deli in the precinct and buy something she really fancies.'

She really was becoming a most accomplished reinforcer, and although not every action had a positive result, there was no doubt that her previous negative lifestyle was changing significantly.

Reinforcing thoughts or fantasies

These are usually part of a semi-formal routine of strengthening the positive, at the expense of negative, moods and feelings. The range of thoughts and fantasies is huge, of course. It can include tunes, rhymes or picture images, indeed any idea or notion that links pleasure to repetition and retrieval and can be easily conjured up at need.

Exercises

- Study the appendix on Cognitive behavioural psychology and read at least one of the recommended texts.

- Using Jacky's case history, make your own short list (ten general items) of reinforcing acts. Incorporate these, as necessary, in your Betterment Programme.

- Make your own short list (five specific items) of reinforcing thoughts and fantasies. Incorporate these, as necessary, in your Betterment Programme.

- Design two charts for monthly completion to record the effectiveness of your listed items in their reinforcement role.

ACTION SITE 9: UNCONSCIOUS MIND

The most significant influence of the unconscious as far as depression is concerned is exerted by the semi-permanent linkage between memories and feelings. Such linkage serves to create an undertow to conscious attitude or expression, develops deeper resonance to thinking and can put a question-mark against exclusively rational, objective appraisals or opinions.

The unconscious is also and necessarily a vital part of the mind's creative apparatus. It provides the conscious, on a bidden or unbidden basis, with a rich range of imagery – symbolic, metaphorical or verbal. It supplies the dream and the day-dream. And it promotes intuitive thinking.

We might expect the unconscious mind to be deeply implicated in the development and maintenance of a depressive state, and our expectation would be justified. Freud and the post-Freudians were especially keen to trace the unconscious causal patterns of their depressive patients. Freud himself linked depressive states with an individual's earliest forgotten episodes of conflict with parents, especially the mother-parent. He also equated depression with mourning and loss, even though the parent might paradoxically be alive!

Berne took the Freudian concept of introjection (the incorporation of parent images, their values, habits, etc., within their children's conscious and unconscious minds) and applied it to the causal mechanisms of depression. He suggested there were sharp and sustained conflicts between introjected parent values and the values of the child, conflicts which might easily extend beyond the parents' actual physical lives and paradoxically *intensify* well after their deaths.

In the psychic battles various roles were played, some of them grotesquely maladroit and inappropriate. Depression resulted from the values of the parent being accepted by the child, and carried into adulthood when he or she was incapable or basically unwilling to live up to them. It was the child's failure then to muster sufficient adult strengths to pursue its own independent and realistic values that sustained the depressive state.

Appeasement strategies

Appeasement recognises the often oppositional and/or unrealistic nature of unconscious thinking or feeling. It accurately senses deeper needs which cannot be met in precise ways because of circumstances, and devises strategies which may help to ease those needs without disaster or unacceptable stress.

Here are examples of appeasement strategies:

- Develop interests that satisfy half-acknowledged needs in realistic, appropriate, ways, e.g. an urge to dominate or control satisfied by involvement in politics.

- Release half-acknowledged or paradoxical urges by means of controlled activities, e.g. suppressed aggression eased by taking up boxing, fencing, judo or squash.

- Act out painful, half-suppressed, distant, personal events either in psychodrama or amateur dramatics.

- Yield to instinctual demands by skilfully planned actions, e.g. job-change, casual sex, personal withdrawal from scene of conflict.

- Attempt the desensitisation of a torturing, obsessive memory by deliberate, scheduled over-recall, thus rendering it less effective.

- Attempt the paradoxical control of disturbing dreams by subjecting them to a formal analysis.

Case history

Pat is a depressed carer who has found an outlet
Pat is a carer, aged 53, unmarried, trying to combine a full-time job with the management of her mother, who has Alzheimer's disease. Even when well, Pat's mother was never the easiest of women; now, gradually becoming demented, she has become an unbelievably capricious, demanding, shell of a person. Pat takes over weekdays at 4pm when the home help leaves. At once her mother goes into high gear, trying to wander off, singing old songs and irritating her daughter intolerably.

Before Pat had an outlet for her urges she was desperate and very depressed. She had never been able to assert herself with her mother since girlhood, and now she was faced with the double stress of coping with an unfulfilled life and the terrible guilt of often wanting to kill her.

But that was before she got into fencing. Pat goes every week-day lunchtime and Sunday morning when she has some respite care. Fencing brings her the following benefits:

- She rids herself of her impulse towards aggression and vague anger.

- She enjoys the competition.

- She makes fresh social contacts.

- She experiences genuine physical fatigue and enhanced appetite.

- She gains some sexual enjoyment when men, occasionally, are introduced to the bouts.

- She also gains satisfaction from developing fresh skills.

- She feels more poised and confident, like Joan of Arc, she says, without the stake!

Challenge strategies
Challenge strategies are altogether rougher and much less compromising. The case history that follows identifies several. In the history they are sequential but they can be separately mounted, if judged appropriate.

Case history

Jack takes the gloves off
Jack had studied Transactional Analysis with some care and had identified a somewhat vague parental command to be perfect. It was probably his father's voice at origin, though he couldn't be quite sure. Of one thing he was certain, it was this command or *injunction* that lay at the root of much of his depression; so, if he were to lift his mood decisively, some action would have to be launched to destroy it.

Jack knew that there were three coping strategies advised for tackling an injunction, namely ignore it, argue with it, or switch it off. He'd tried to ignore it, but without much success. The technique for arguing proposed that one put the commanding parent before one in imagination and challenged their assertions. So Jack conjured up a vivid picture of his father and asked him, 'Why has it got to be perfect, Dad?' 'Because your employers demand it,' answered his Dad. 'I've news for you, Dad,' Jack said, 'my employers couldn't care less about perfection. They're not making Rolls Royces, they're making profits.' 'That may well be,' Dad retorted, 'but in the end they're bound to come round to my views.' 'In the end we're all dead, as you yourself are, Dad,' Jack said. 'There's no guarantee that dotting the Is and crossing the Ts will get me anywhere. Far better to be a rough and ready man and move on to more promising projects.'

And so the argument continued; and Jack persisted with the technique for some weeks. But he had to admit that Dad and his doctrine still kept surfacing. So, as a last resort, he decided to try the switching-off tactic. There were various methods of thought-stopping advocated but Jack chose the tape-recorded version. This involved asking a neighbour to record Dad's favourite perfectionist naggings on an audio cassette, playing these over, and then switching them off. The next phase was to build up the mental image of the tape-recorder so that it could be brought into the mind's eye at any time, preferably at those times when Dad's perfectionist nonsense was just about to surface. As soon as there was the slightest hint, Jack centred the image and then supplemented it with another of his hand extending and switching the recorder off.

It was this third method that finally rid Jack of Dad and put some limit on the self-undermining thoughts that Dad powered, and which had gone a long way to sustaining Jack's depressive moods.

Exercises

Define an unconscious target as clearly as you can. This may not be easy and you may need to look deeply inside yourself, note passing thoughts and try to remember your dreams. Describe your target – a painful memory, parental injunction, guilty recollection, deep need, etc. It's best to write it down but destroy this written record when you have succeeded in appeasing or challenging it.

Then decide on an appropriate appeasement strategy to direct at your target. Plan and implement it thoroughly using the appendices and other sections of the book. After a six month trial, record any mood improvement and persist if improvement is noticeable. If no improvement is discernable, attempt a second appeasement strategy and should this not succeed, move to challenge.

For challenge, particularly if specific parental injunctions are involved, you will need precise statements both for recording and visualisation purposes. These will have to be built up into dialogues as appropriate. You will also probably need dramatising help from discreet friends.

ACTION SITE 10: SLEEPING AND PRESLEEPING

Several characteristic sleep disturbances are closely associated with depression. Sleep disturbances can be divided into two categories:

- Difficulty in dropping off to sleep. There may be several factors causing this, but prominent amongst them is obsessive or depressive thinking which activates the sufferer.

- Early waking and failure to regain sleep within a reasonable period. Here also several factors may be contributory but, once again, obsessive or depressive thoughts tend to dominate the sufferer and keep him or her awake.

Either or both of these can occur in the same depression, together with several other types of sleep upset, all of which we shall examine in detail.

Sleeping frame of mind
It's especially vital to be in a positive frame of mind about sleeping. Sleep must not be thought of as an unreliable and superfluous interval, but as a life-enhancing, restorative, rhythm-providing, problem-solving state, much to be respected and sought. Good sound sleeping depends as much, if not more, on events and attitudes before retiring as on the actual process itself.

Presleeping
The presleeping period, or the events which foreshadow and immediately precede sleeping, are crucial and manipulable. An improving mood which has been on a steady upward or stable optimistic line since midday may begin to dip as the prospects of sleep approach. There can be several interwoven reasons for this: a downward trend in bodily rhythm or revival of memories of sleeplessness may both tend to depress mood.

This means that the presleeping period is as critical as any during the day and requires as much care. Specifically, it is the time for the depressive to avoid all links or contacts which renew depressive associations. Watching a significant television play, reading a particular book or allowing a conversation to veer towards depressive topics are examples of dangerous activities and must in all circumstances be avoided.

Sleep has to be approached with a positive attitude based on *regular retiring times*, with all anti-sleeping influences in terms of thoughts and perceptions excluded.

The bedroom and its meanings
Most sensible people sleep in a bedroom, but they often muddle the meanings and purpose of that room. Bedrooms double up as workshops, offices, canteens or theatres offering a range of often conflicting usages and a confusion of meanings. It is within such

confusions that sleep problems often partly lie. Sleep is an instinctually and socially conditioned response to sleep-inducing cues, which ideally are simple, consistent and regular. The message is clear. Bedrooms that supply *counter-sleeping cues* require total revamping. Bedrooms are for sleep, sex, illness and for *nothing else*. So, out with all extraneous fittings – telephones, computers, television sets, etc. These present a range of cue-confusions which can do you no service at all in your drive for cue-clarity. Bedrooms, to fulfil their role, need a single coherent image which can condition sleep reliably. Nothing else will do.

Comfort and silence

Beds have to be comfortable and bedrooms quiet. Poor sleepers who share beds should consider sleeping on their own, ideally in the same room as their partners. Poor sleep is infectious, and almost impossible to remedy if the rhythms of a partner need to be considered. Partners may also vary greatly in their tolerance of heat and cold, making shared bedclothes a complication. Big, single beds of divan type offer the best chance of solving sleeping difficulties. Comfort by continuous rolling is obtainable, and tumbling out not a serious problem.

Silence, if not golden, is at least silver in bedrooms. It need not be absolute, but if noise cannot be kept down, double-glazing should be considered. When regular nocturnal sounds like milk-deliveries cannot be suppressed, the bedroom must be changed. Bird noise may also have to be avoided by a room change.

Light, and an excess of it, can also present difficulties in bedrooms. Early morning waking may often be cued to the dawn which needs to be kept out, as do street lights. Only heavy curtains with tightly-fitted pelmets will exclude light and these will certainly be required if waking becomes conditioned to light.

Sleep-gaining techniques

One crucial sleep-disturber in older men is the cold-erection. This is not so much a rouser in its own right but a trigger for urination which sends the victim to the toilet and thereafter keeps him awake. Cold-erections (they are distinguishable from nocturnal emissions) can be kept in check by regular intercourse, mastur-bation and, even in the worst case, by sleeping without pyjama trousers. Without the snag of material there is a good chance that a cold-erection may subside by itself without rousing its owner.

Cold-erections lead naturally on to considering problems of nocturnal urination, generally. Urgency (need to go) and frequency (how often) can sometimes be symptoms of physical bladder ailments in both men and women. If examination excludes a physical cause, a psychological attack needs to be made on the problem because, otherwise, sleep can be ruined.

Going to bed with a full bladder is clearly not sensible and it is better to drink the bulk of necessary daily fluids in the morning and early afternoon to ensure that you are 'drained down' at bedtime. Time spent on urination before settling down is never wasted. Better to take five minutes in the toilet than run the risk of being roused twice during the night.

False bladder cues during the night can sometimes be overridden by rolling on to one's back, thus taking the pressure off the sender system. Commanding oneself to banish urgency may also sometimes work. Routines such as counting to 30, at which number the urgency will have faded, may be effective, but to work best they need to have been practised during the day.

If urgency does succeed in forcing a toilet visit, it is very useful and feasible to manage this in the dark. Before moving it is always wise to check your orientation but when you are satisfied, the entire trip should be a smooth, sleepy, manoeuvre through half-opened doors accompanied by a stream of self-assurances such as, 'As soon as I get back to bed I shall fall asleep', or 'This is the only time I shall get up tonight'.

However, you may not drop off to sleep after such an arousal and, indeed, slipping into sleep may not generally be very easy. For this problem we recommend various routines:

- Drowsy imagery – see the appendix on Relaxation and pleasure for details.

- Thought-stopping – this technique, discussed in detail in Action Site 3, seeks to block arousal thinking.

- Masturbation – occasionally can be effective in cases of sexual frustration.

- Modelling posture – this is simply adopting a life-long, preferred sleeping position, focusing on lying side, head angle, height of bedclothes, adjustment of arms and legs, etc.

There are several points to note about dreams and dreaming. Generally, dreams and especially nightmares, are not good news for poor sleepers, *but you should note that waking from a dream is evidence that at least an hour and possibly more has elapsed since you were previously awake.* At the start of a night this can be a powerful reinforcing thought. 'I have been asleep once, and I can sleep again.'

Exercise and sleep

Nobody, whether depressed or not, can expect to sleep properly without *sufficient* and *appropriate* exercise. There must be enough exercise and of the correct kind to establish and sustain good sleeping patterns.

Less than two miles of quick walking can be judged insufficient daily exercise for fit adults. But games or sports with great emphasis on reflex action and speed, like badminton, squash of ice-hockey, should *not* be played in the two hours before going to bed.

Nightmares

Nightmares and their consequences need to be managed in depression for two important reasons. First they are sleep disturbances in their own right and can seriously upset patterns of rest. Second, they may have after effects, colouring mood the next day. A good drill for the immediate aftermath of a nightmare is to sit up or visit the toilet, using this two- or three-minute period to re-establish personal reality. Next, self-assurance must be regained using unvoiced statements like:

'That's not real and never could be real.'

'There's something in that dream which might be useful, if I think about it during the day.'

'One reassuring feature of a nightmare is the speed I get off to sleep again after it.'

'I will not have another nightmare tonight.'

'I shall sleep more soundly as a result of this nightmare.'

'Should I have another nightmare tonight or in future I will try to wake up before it reaches its frightening peak.'

'The more my nightmares run to a pattern in content, the more skilful I shall be at breaking into them and waking up relatively calm.'

'As I grow less depressed, so my nightmares will become fewer until they occur only very rarely and manageably.'

'It is my depression and the fact that nightmares happen in the vulnerable early hours that makes them seem more serious than they really are.'

Case history

Alan really gets to grips with the problem
Alan was going through a very depressed period and his sleep was much disturbed. It would frequently take him more than two hours to drop off when he climbed into bed and there was no doubt that anxiety about sleep was increasing the misery of the day. He began to feel that if he could only get on top of his sleeping problem, then an alleviation of his ordinary stresses might follow. 'At least,' he said to himself, 'if I could guarantee myself seven hours sleep a night, I might be able to generate sufficient confidence to see my other difficulties in better proportion.' The big problem was that as soon as he put out the light, all his troubles returned to torment him and seemed twice as big as during the daytime.

As with all attempts at self-management, the first need was for an overall assessment of his sleeping. He had geared himself up to being quite good at analysing problems and this was so important that he felt he must analyse it right to its depths. Thinking about it indicated that he was always chopping and changing his time of going to bed: frequently there were two hour variations. Secondly, he was often depressed and tense when he went to bed, and, thirdly, like many problem-sleepers, he continued to worry persistently long after his head had touched the pillow.

He determined on a two- or three-pronged assault on his problem and the first prong was a definite attack through stimulus control. It seemed likely that some part of his physical environment was associated with his poor sleep and, although he wasn't able to identify precisely all the particular stimuli, he decided to alter the physical arrangements within his bedroom as much as possible by putting the bed in another part of the room, facing in a different direction and changing the furniture and decoration as far as it was financially practicable. Then he decided to fix on a bedtime and awakening time and hold to them as though they were a schedule, so that every moment of the day, in a sense, was keyed in with them.

He also decided to break all other associations of the bedroom with non-sleeping. He had frequently played CDs in his bedroom but he discontinued this habit and used the sitting-room instead. The tactic was to make the bedroom associated only with sleep-compatible behaviour. Next he reduced as far as he possibly could any distracting stimuli. There was a lot of light from flickering neon signs nearby, so he doubled up the curtain thickness and put a piece of acrylic over the window which could be clipped in temporarily to keep out some of the traffic noise. There was cheap carpet felt about and he managed to pad the floor to a depth of another inch so as to keep down some of the noise from the flats underneath. Additionally, he made sure that under no circumstances (not always very easy) did he take any naps during the day.

Finally, he was absolutely determined to make a specific attack on all the intrusive worrying thoughts that came to him as soon as his head had touched the pillow, and decided to establish one place and one specific time in the early part of the evening for worrying about next day's events. Indeed, he made this worry period very constructive in the sense that he would attempt future problem-solving. He was also determined that he would not carry on with the rest of the evening's activities or go to bed before he had performed this specific worry activity. He chose as a worry period the half-hour after he had cooked and eaten his supper and before he went out to enjoy himself in the evening.

Meanwhile he developed progressive relaxation training for himself. There were three reasons why he was keen to do this. First, he knew that progressive relaxation was very effective in cutting off the worrying thoughts and images that had hitherto disturbed his sleep. Second, the very fact of concentrating upon relaxation gave him a particular internal stimulus on which he could focus his attention. In this way it supplied him with a behaviour that was completely incompatible with any other kind of sleep disturbance. Third, progressive relaxation schemes made him more alert, vigorous and confident during the day when he carried them out.

His progressive relaxation involved the systematic tensing and releasing of various muscle systems throughout the body and the directing of attention to the sensation which resulted from this. At first, he involved himself in training sessions lasting some 45 minutes, and he practised the procedure daily. As he practised, he became more and more successful at producing feelings of deep relaxation and finally after about ten weeks of daily practice he could relax himself on command. Finally, he felt able to go to bed and bid himself to relax in much the same way as he had taught himself during the day without necessarily going through all the muscle relaxation and contraction routine. It wasn't long before his sleeping problems began to respond to this multi-pronged strategy. He found himself increasingly able to drop off within ten or 15 minutes of his head touching the pillow, and there began to be occasions when he hardly remembered even climbing into bed.

Exercises
Construct your own management checklist, incorporating points from:

- sleeping frame of mind

- bedroom and its meanings

- comfort and silence

- sleeping techniques

but introducing items which fit *your* particular circumstances. Use the checklist to decide your sleeping strategy and chart your progress.

6

Building an Individual Betterment Programme

There is no doubt that the ten Action Sites, to say nothing of the Appendix references, are a formidable challenge. But they do provide essential leverage points to open up your state of mind to betterment programmes of your own devising.

CASE HISTORIES

Charles devises a betterment programme with a unifying theme

Charles, whose Action Site priority choices had been Waking thoughts and feelings, Looking forward and Sleeping and presleeping, was a physical chap with something of an economical turn of mind. So, it was not surprising that he sought to make sport and exercise common elements in his betterment programme. The biggest problem with his depression was waking up, almost always after a disturbed night, with dreadful feelings of despair and fright. These had been particularly dire after his partner of 18 months had walked out and, if anything, were worsening. 'If I don't tackle them somehow,' Charles said to himself, 'one of these far from fine mornings, they are going to find me hanging from the banisters.'

The Action Site recommended action and Charles interpreted this as a suggestion to jog. 'I will count 40 from when the radio-alarm goes off,' Charles said, 'and then I will put my trainers on, grab my keys and get jogging.'

Getting jogging was most difficult the first time he tried it. He practically had to haul himself out of bed, groaning with reluctant despair. But the second morning it was easier and he went further, even though it started to pour with rain. By the end of a fortnight, a routine had become established. He was running at least two miles, showering as soon as he returned and microwaving for himself something really tasty for breakfast to cope with his increased appetite. He kept a weekly record of his morning mood and noticed that by the end of the third week he was pushing the morning gloom aside within minutes. It was being replaced by a real eagerness to cover distance and a keenness to establish a running rhythm.

Looking forward was his second Action Site and the sports theme helped him here. Charles played squash twice a week, on the men's ladder on Tuesdays and the mixed ladder on Thursdays. Almost immediately the mixed ladder created a holding interest for him in the shape (in both senses) of a young woman who was climbing it fast. Within a month he had played her twice and had a drink with her at the centre bar.

As far as anticipated pleasure went, he had put his name down for a wacky-sounding Ball Week. Players were to stay at a local hostel and were given the chance of professional coaching in five ball games. 'At the end of the week we shall either be knackered or crippled,' Charles said to himself, 'but, and this is important, it's something to look forward to and, if I get a chance, I might point it out to that girl at the squash club.'

The final Action Site was Sleeping and presleeping. Charles was certain that he was having sufficient physical exercise to make him sleep and was taking care not to play squash after seven in the evening. But that still left him with a real problem of getting to sleep and staying asleep. Charles did everything the Action Site suggested in respect of bedroom fittings and environment. Then he determined to go for broke in terms of relaxation. 'What I want,' he said, 'is a sure-fire method of calming myself down to zero, which I can turn on at will, any time the need presents itself, namely, getting to sleep and early waking.'

Charles studied not only the relaxation schemes in the appendix on Relaxation and pleasure, but also several other routines published in self-help books. Eventually he decided on visualisation as the best model. He'd always been fond of Robert Bridges' magic poem 'London Snow'. Ever since childhood he had been entranced, not only by its rhythms, but also the images of falling and accumulating that it could produce. He persuaded his sister to record 'London Snow' for him on a continuous tape cassette. It was this that he listened to (the recorder on a ten-minute timer) just after going to bed and it was this that he deliberately recited to himself, if he woke during the night. His plan was to try to condition sleeping to the stimulus of the poem, so that it would mesh with all the other sleep-inducing cues that the bedroom provided. The process certainly needed persistence but, as week followed week, the conditioning strengthened steadily and by the end of three months the poem was becoming a reliable way of both bringing and maintaining sleep. 'I'm especially pleased at the way it can usually get me off again,' Charles congratulated himself. 'It stops me fretting and that's a big bonus.'

Of course, Charles did not lose sight of the fact that this focus on and relative success with three priority Action Sites amounted to a very good beginning but not a complete conquest of his depression. There were two more sites with lesser but still significant priorities for tackling, so he was not complacent. 'But I've gone a fair distance,' he congratulated himself. 'And built up a level of confidence that will serve me well as I face those two next challenges.'

Useful features to note in Charles' betterment programme

- He sets realistic aims for himself and either assesses progress on his own account or lets others (the squash ladders) do it for him.

- He is economical with resources and keeps to what he knows.

- He builds on activities and grasps opportunities (sex contacts at the sports centre and events advertised).

- He does not hesitate to use childhood reassurance ('London Snow') when this is appropriate.

Alison's betterment programme is rooted in straight thinking

Straight thinking had always been Alison's aim, so it was to be expected that her Action Site priority choices of Other upsets, Upswings and Unconscious mind would reflect both that aim and the way she hoped to tackle the exercises on the sites.

She was certainly in persistent difficulties with several of the depressive thought take-overs which she read about in Other upsets. Take what was termed personalising. She was cruelly prone to it, constantly interpreting happenings and remarks as if they were directed at or exclusively concerned her and almost always seeming to be a victim.

But now that she realised what was happening and could put a name to the process, there was more than a chance it could be controlled. So she developed a drill to cope with it. Each time she felt the urge to personalise, she said to herself, 'Stop, you are starting to personalise. Wait before you conclude you are the target. What is your evidence? You are going to need more evidence than that. Why should you be the target? The target might be somebody else; there probably isn't a target at all.'

This drill was valuable in several ways. First of all it gave her time to decide how to react, observe and weigh evidence – all valuable phases in the process of controlling her reactions, and shaping her responses. She quickly learned to be sensitive to the special situations in which she was prone to personalise (with certain people, in particular circumstances) and then she found she could grade her response accordingly.

For example, the simplest situation was the staff-restaurant stare (when she imagined everyone was looking at her at the counter). Commands to herself, with a half-glance around at the till, showed her that nobody was watching her at all. They were all too busy stuffing their faces in the limited lunch-time allowed, she concluded.

As for other events which seemed to have her label on them, she became very adept at relabelling. 'It could refer to anybody', or 'It doesn't mean anything', were typical of the relabelling phrases she shot at herself whenever she sensed a label coming into view.

As regards upswings, Alison was even more decisively single-minded. There were three self-commands for every upswing, she reminded herself:

- Discover and note what, if anything, caused it.

- While it lasts make the most of it.

- Try to ensure that, if possible, it happens again soon.

These three meant she had to be alert and ready with a kit of actions whenever an upswing took place. Take, for instance, the morning upswing she found herself experiencing in the middle of one of the most terrifying thunderstorms ever to hit the city. There were hailstones the size of marbles; it was a mercy the office windows held. Alison realised, for the first time, that her mood could change paradoxically and, though one could not rely on thunderstorms, external events might be useful.

Myra had run out screaming because of the thunder, so Alison followed her into the Ladies and held her for at least ten minutes. Miss Caxton hunted them down and seemed most relieved that Alison had been so supportive. When the thunderstorm had passed she'd come over to Alison and said 'We're looking for a departmental first-aider. There's only one increment in it, but I'll put your name forward, if you like.' 'Yes please, I would,' Alison said.

That was a very clever reinforcing move, as she realised later. It meant that she had status, which is always good for morale but, more important, each time the necessary training or drills came round, she could reasonably anticipate some kind of upswing.

Alison was also just coming to realise that being determinedly single made her a hostage to all kinds of impulses from the unconscious mind and one of the most pressing in her case was the need to nurture and cherish. So where could she find a satisfactory object for all the caring instincts that were so strong inside her? She cast around, studying the local press and, then, quite by chance, she happened on an advertisement for volunteers to launch an animal-rescue charity. Within a matter of months, she had graduated from running jumble sales to driving the rescue van, three hours an evening every other weekday.

From the Leisure counselling reference in the appendix, Alison realised that her rescue work, with all the emotions that charged it, was a release activity that she was following, half-unknowingly. When she was eventually co-opted onto the steering committee with all the extra responsibilities that entailed, all her possible outlets seemed to be completely filled and she felt fully satisfied for the first time in her life.

She was not complacent though. Three Action Sites had shown crucial improvement but her betterment programme was by no means complete. There were two other close priority Action Sites to be tackled and a whole lifestyle to be progressively re-adjusted.

Useful features to note in Alison's Betterment Programme

- She is highly systematic, moving into programme actions that yield progressive and easy to assess possibilities.

- She grabs immediate opportunities or works hard to create them when they are not immediately available.

- She is prepared to revolutionise her life, if this will serve her needs.

- She realises that a good beginning is not the equivalent of a satisfactory ending.

7

Staying Well

For a recovered depressive there is nothing accidental, providential or inevitable about staying well. Staying well is not easy; it requires courage, energy and judgement. But the good news is that staying well is a whole dimension simpler than getting better and the reason for this difference lies in the gaining of insight.

VALUING INSIGHT

What is insight? Insight is knowledge deepened by experience; for the average recovered depressive it offers a sharpened understanding of the predisposing factors and best methods of tackling the former ailment. Such insight is dearly bought, but much prized. This is especially the case for those who have recovered with the help of the kind of approaches outlined in this book. Their recovery has been systematically facilitated, meaning that the insights gained are easily retrieved and, if necessary, reapplied because they are set within a framework.

STAYING FREE OF DEPRESSION

In reality you cannot expect necessarily to be entirely free of depression in future. But if you follow certain preventive guidelines there is an excellent prospect of your being able to sustain level moods for long periods while being alert to the kinds of change in yourself and your circumstances which may threaten renewed depressive episodes.

- **Psycho- and bio-regularity** Maintaining an informal chart overview of psycho-rhythms (sleep, sex, etc) and bio-rhythms (appetite, energy etc) will give us advance warning of changes significant for future depressive onsets.

- **Orientation** This defines our relationship with the changing world. We need to maintain a sense of personal momentum as well as direction, and couple these with feelings of belonging and familiarity. Should we experience unease with our orientation, it may indicate an intimate vacuum which depressive thinking may easily penetrate. Connection with events and especially others is everything.

- **Hobbies, activities and interests** You must maintain and adjust and enhance these, especially if they originally were the foundation on which you based your recovery from depression. You must not permit them to be downgraded by others or allow others to dictate your enjoyment of them.

- **Confiding relationships** It is vital to retain at least one secure, confiding, relationship. This needs to be with someone who is patient, non-judgemental, not necessarily deeply involved, but reliable and available.

- **Strategic sense** This is the ability to stand back, take stock, assess strengths and weaknesses and recall old reliable ways of reacting. You need to keep this sense because no life can be guaranteed free of depression-making events, sometimes severe and unanticipated. When such events happen their impacts may be severe, but if we have kept our strategic sense and rational-emotive control over our feelings, they will not be decisively depressing.

- **Personal avoidance list** Do not risk unnecessarily any stimuli which past experience indicates tend to depress you. Depressives simply must not expose themselves to such events, and must compile not only their own avoidance lists, but also the range of tactics best suited to evading them in part or totally. Such lists will differ from person to person, naturally. Some will avoid funerals or hospitals, for instance, unless absolutely compelled, others steer clear of situations where assessment is likely or scrutiny by others, probable.

It's worthwhile making occasional charts to keep track of any changes in these six freedom domains. Such a record needs no formal scheme; a simple monthly note is all that is necessary for maintaining alertness and generating remedial action. See Monthly Freedom Chart (page 84).

Monthly Freedom Chart

A	B	C	D	E	F
Psycho- and bio-regularity	**Orientation**	**Hobbies, activities or interests**	**Confiding relationships**	**Strategic sense**	**Personal avoidance list**
Chart specifically any rhythms that seem to be varying outside normal limits.	Describe your current feelings of momentum, belonging and familiarity.	State the degree of your involvement in specific hobbies, activities or interests and note any attempts to deepen such involvement.	Note any change in the strength of confiding relationships, and action taken to remedy any weakness.	Describe how you maintain your strategic sense in relation to possible events.	Write your list and note any instances of avoidance or forced exposure.

FOR THE ACTION-MINDED READER

If you are proactively inclined, you may wish to build up your own staying-well programmes. We suggest you work within the following three issues, developing each along the lines instructed in the earlier part of the book and also drawing upon the wide range of appendix material. *Particularly recommended is the appendix on Decision-making in depression.*

Maintaining a balanced lifestyle

There are natural self-righting elements in the mind which are probably decisive in lifting a depression. But they do require the long-term support of a balanced lifestyle if they are to be kept in a state of working readiness. Such a balance cannot be a partial, selective process; it ought to be an across-the-board function, involving all body-mind activities in equilibrium-seeking.

Anticipating life-changes

Thinking about the inevitable changes that time will bring in the roles we play and our styles of life may be a frightening, even depressing, experience. But the result of *not* considering such changes, of even denying they will occur, can be hugely demoralising when the impacts of the inevitable arrive.

Anticipating and its implications
Planning and desensitisation are interdependent and essential for anticipating. Planning comprises all that is feasible in terms of future preparation; it is an administrative function, probably involving others. Desensitisation, however, is a deeply emotive and individual form of preliminary rehearsal of future reactions. Neither is a precise technique for the obvious reason that the future and one's response to it are not precisely predictable. But both are vital elements in this action site.

Nursing individuality

As we emphasised in the first chapter, it is all too easy in these days of information overload and pressure to conform, for the individual to lose his or her intimate values, standards and sense of personal worthiness.

There is but one way to withstand the depression-making impacts of all this pressure and that is to build up your own incredulity kit. This is a set of phrases ready for use when your standards, values or preferences are under threat. Here is a far from complete range:

> 'Haven't I heard something like this before?'
> 'I expected him or her to say that.'
> 'What am I meant to conclude?'
> 'Do I need it?'
> 'Why should I believe it?'
> 'Does it refer to me?'
> 'What is it in aid of?'
> 'Am I being pressured?'
> 'There's a bandwagon starting to roll.'
> 'It's persuasively argued, but . . .'

Appendix 1

Decisions in Depression

Broadly the message of this appendix is to warn against taking any significant decision while a depressive state lasts, and to be wary about decisions that others close to us may be contemplating if they seem to be in a similar condition.

This advice is not meant to lock you into endless ruminations about whether a decision is significant or not. Broadly, a significant decision is one that has consequences that cannot easily be reversed – of the job-changing, house-moving, partner-leaving category. We also need to clarify the depth of depression we are talking about. It must be moderate to deep. Duration also is important here; if a depression is more than a two or three day mood, then it qualifies for wariness, especially if the decision is a vital one.

Why do we need to be careful about deciding while we are depressed? The reason lies in distortions of perception, reasoning, memory and emotion that may be detrimental to good choosing.

The elements of a decision are:

- **aim** – what we hope the decision will achieve

- **information** – the data we need on which to base our decision

- **evaluation** – the tests we apply to judge the reliability of such data

- **decision** – the precise timing and act of choosing between alternatives.

Depression can be dynamically destructive in several ways:

- **Aim:** it can be difficult, if not impossible to focus clearly on objectives. A depression seriously affects your sense of proportion and orientation, leading to distorted attitudes; all undermining clear aims.

- **Information:** a depression may seriously interfere with the amount of information acquired (too little or too much) and also cause its acquisition to be critically unselective.

- **Evaluation:** this skill can be much compromised in depression, which undermines mental and emotive judgement to varying degrees.

- **Decision:** the act itself, and its important timing, can be upset by impulse or hesitation, irrationally driven.

THE BOTTOM LINE IN DEFERRED DECISIONS

If you recognise that your decision is important while at the same time your depression is disabling, your safest course is to *move into deferral mode* without delay. It may not be easy explaining or arranging deferral; others may put pressure on you; you may even be threatened in various ways with penalties. But such embarrassments are small-scale when set against the potential future calamities of making a wrong choice.

MOOD ALLOWANCE

Developed sensitivity to the influence of depressive mood on decisions and choices is called mood allowance. As previously outlined, deciding depends on complex information-processing in which emotion plays a significant part. As it is a conscious process, there is always the opportunity to judge the varying impact of mood on decisions, and, if such judgements are based on experience, to make allowances for variations in mood-states. In the short case-history to follow, we show how it is possible to use developed insight to make such necessary adjustments.

Case history

Jeremy makes allowances for his mood
'I'm depressed,' Jeremy concluded, 'not deeply depressed, and not likely to remain depressed for long but, as of this moment, that is what I am. Mind you, I see positive aspects, or rather an aspect; I've developed a sound awareness of how depressed I am, and can separate two realities; in other words I know what normal is, and that I'm not there at this time. I have to be careful in this state; I must remind myself that decisions are particularly prone to be

influenced by moods. So, I can do two things about any decision. I can put it off until my mood changes, and even make my depression the excuse. I can say that I'm not in the right frame of mind, or words to that effect. On the other hand, if I'm really confident I can, if necessary, make a careful choice and allow for my mood. Which I'll only do if I absolutely have to. It's not simple. You have to picture yourself in a normal state of mind with normal hopes and expectations. This is how you should act, not how you feel like acting, and it's far from easy making the right adjustments. But sometimes it's the only course open to me. I have to ask myself what my normal view of facts and outcomes is. Luckily, I remember what it is, despite my feelings at the moment.'

CONTRA-INDICATIONS TO DECISION-MAKING (DANGER TIME)

If you are suffering from any of the ailments or conditions described below, resist the urge to decide important issues regardless of external or internal pressures on you. Take refuge in deferral, procrastination, sloth or downright bloody-mindedness, and put off choosing until you feel, and preferably others confirm, that the phase has passed.

- **Post-traumatic stress states** – these follow accidents or profound shocks. They can be long-lasting, and sometimes recurrent.

- **Bereavement sequels** – these periods of mourning hold particular decision-making dangers. Temporary delusions about the deceased's wishes or desires to recompense the dead can destroy judgement.

- **Post-operative periods** – the risk here lies not so much in the physical shock of an operation but in the psychological consequences of anaesthetics. These can produce profound, but not always recognisable, personality changes that can take months to readjust or stabilise.

- **Post-influenza conditions** – influenza is especially crucial, but all high fevers are potentially dangerous. Certain influenza virus strains can leave a sufferer with severe depression or anxiety, or both. After the inertia the illness brings, *there may also be a paradoxical drive to take action.*

- **Seasonal affective disorder (SAD)** – this typically begins in November or early December as the hours of daylight decrease. At the beginning, the symptoms resemble influenza with aching joints followed by an intense, generalised feeling of irritability. The sufferer experiences sensations of cold; shivering bouts are common and depression grows. Weight-gain distinguishes SAD from depression, in which weight stays steady or is lost.

- **Post-natal depression** – childbirth is an emotional and usually a traumatic time. Many mothers experience low moods, which may persist for several weeks. A minority develop much severer depressions or other forms of mental illness – these need professional help.

Appendix 2

Self-esteem

In fully-developed depression, self-esteem suffers almost by definition. But it is possible to lose one's self-respect, and fail to regain it for long periods without being markedly depressed. Serious and sustained loss of self-esteem is not, however, a pleasant state of living; great bitterness and disruption of close relationships can ensue as well as various compensatory, addictive behaviours.

Loss of self-esteem occurs when we meet with an event that directly, indirectly or symbolically undermines our belief in ourselves. It can only happen if we are self-involved with such events *in the special sense of our personal prestige*. Other kinds of happenings may depress us, but not damage our self-image.

We may suffer depression-making bereavements for instance without loss of self-esteem, but should we be sacked from a job to which we have given our all, or witness the defeat of a cause or group we have made our own, then our self-confidence and belief will inevitably suffer a substantial blow.

Checklist on self-esteem

- Remember that levels of self-esteem rise and fall, sometimes rapidly.

- Remember that raising one's self-esteem is essential in lifting depression.

- Realise that self-esteem can usually be regained *despite* external events, if you take action.

- Understand that regaining self-esteem involves recovering original satisfactions and using these to reinforce present positive moods.

- Understand that maintaining self-esteem often hangs on an ability to control and reshape memory, and to marshal effective rationalisations or compensations for negative episodes in our past lives.

THREE BROAD TYPES OF SELF-ESTEEM LOSS

- **Short-term**, when the loss is soon regained either by change of circumstances or a successful retrieval technique.

- **Long-term**, in which measures to sustain self- esteem will need to be durable and consistently taken.

- **Crisis**, coping with severe, very demoralising and not easily negotiable crisis-losses may only be possible via drastic life-style changes.

The following three case histories feature somewhat different self-esteem retrieval strategies. Colin's is a brief damage-limitation exercise, launched to cope with depression-inducing impacts of unexpected events. Kate, by contrast, has been in-volved in half a lifetime's successful battle with the fall-out from early failure, a disaster which she soon recognised had to be rationalised and minimised if she were to keep up her morale and self-confidence. Tim has an esteem problem of quite a different dimension, requiring massive lifestyle changes.

CASE HISTORY

Colin regains his self-esteem

Looking back, Colin recognised that the deplorable state of his window-sills had probably saved him from a deep depression. Five of them, two upstairs, had almost rotted away. So around Christmas he got an estimate and received a shock – he job would cost nearly a thousand pounds. A sum like that would have made a man in work think twice, but Colin was soon not in work; three weeks into the new year he was made redundant. February and March were a sorry record of failed interviews (Colin had never been a good interviewee) so by April he was both disconsolate and becoming strapped for money. It was plain that Colin and his wife would have to sell their house in the spring. But the sills were immensely off-putting. They had now rotted so badly that ragged edges gaped as if something had eaten the woodwork. As Colin gazed at them he was filled with despair; his confidence in himself and his belief that somehow his luck would change had shrunk to virtually nothing. It was then that he suddenly, and quite unaccountably, decided to try to repair the sills himself.

Colin had never been a handyman. His late father's tools were stacked in the garden shed. Colin's father, a man given to hurtful remarks, had said that his son was both cack-handed and bucky-fisted, comments calculated to put a child off tool-use for a lifetime.

It was hard work, but with the help of the local timber merchants and his wife, Colin managed to fix them – and make a good job of it.

Gazing up at his handiwork Colin was filled with a strange new pride. 'You were wrong about me,' he said under his breath to his father. 'And what's more Dad, you're dead.'

A month later they sold the house, and cut their running expenses by a third. A month after that Colin found another job. It only paid half his previous earnings, but it was a job. They asked him at the interview if he could help out with maintenance. 'Of course, I've just fixed the sills on my house,' said Colin.

Exercises for self-esteem building (short-term loss)
If you have experienced event-related damage to your self-esteem review an earlier hobby, activity or interest for:

- aspects you've never explored

- feasible challenges within such aspects

- fresh but attainable skills to meet such challenges.

Then break new ground with your old interest, and allow that success to reinforce your confidence in general.

CASE HISTORY

Kate defends her self-esteem
Kate had several weapons to aid her in keeping her self-confidence. Her principal aid to empowerment was rationalisation. Despite the undeniable memory that she had once spent two years at drama school but had subsequently never been offered more than a handful of walk-on parts, the failure did not get to her as it might have done. There were prompts enough though. One of her former fellow students was now an enormous star, never out of the theatrical spotlight. If Kate hadn't developed a sixth sense for avoiding seeing him on television, film

or in the Sunday supplements, she would have been forced into 'might-have-beens'. But she was too busy with her boutique, an ailing husband and two adolescent children to bother with the theatre. 'I can't imagine why I was ever interested in the theatre,' Kate said to herself. 'Must have been my over-extended adolescence.' Her main hobby was gardening. She grew, very expertly, flowers for the shop, and vegetables for the kitchen.

All in all, Kate had fought a successful lifetime's 'stopping battle'. She had not meekly 'come to terms' with her failure. By contrast, she had accomplished a revolution in personal values which had transformed her aims.

Developing long-term character armour

If you are experiencing a return of self-doubt, stimulated by memories of past failure:

- List your personal successes.

- List the success of any movement or idea you have supported.

- Note where prompts and cues to your past failure occur, and take care to avoid them.

- Switch off self-denigrating memories or ideas.

- Find some hobby, activity or interest to distract you from tormenting thoughts.

- While keeping closely tuned to present needs, review areas of past interest and competence with a view to regaining more general morale by recovering old skills.

- Recognise that present loss of self-esteem may relate to very early experiences of being either devalued or not valued for oneself.

- Try to keep all fresh challenges realistic; make your objectives achievable.

- Develop a set of self-esteem building mantras. 'That which does not destroy me, makes me strong', etc.

So far we have focused on best cases. But what of those whose self-esteem has been shattered, and whose lives have no firm prospects of mending? How will they sustain belief in themselves?

The tentative (it cannot be other) answer lies in the very tightly-programmed life-style that our final character has fashioned for himself. This is Tim's detailed and intimate diary. Note the numbers in the text. These refer to the ten-point list of essential activities that follow the diary.

CASE HISTORY

Tim tries to sustain some self-esteem

6.30 am   Up and out of the house silently, so as not to disturb the wife. A very gentle mile jog, gentle lest I wear down my trainers, and have to resort to rubber patches, but strenuous enough to shift my depression on waking. Were I to stop in bed I would certainly fret. As it is, I blow those early morning blues away with action. (1 and 3)

7.15 am   I'm back, showered and started on cooking breakfast; the wife has still to show. My contribution to breakfast is minimal, at the moment; bread for the toast. Hens are still not feasible on the allotment on account of foxes and vandals, but I'm considering ways of keeping them surreptitiously here at home in our pocket-handkerchief sized garden. (9)

8.30 am   The wife is away in the car, which is affordable since I got made redundant only because I have managed to overcome my inhibitions and actually service it. Fortunately she drives it gently and has not, up till now, bent it. Should this happen, it would open up a whole new era of mechanical challenges. I wash up and tidy round.

9.15 am   I set off on my bicycle for the library, which is where I do most of my studying. It's not the most ideal of places (I could stay at home) but I feel I need the stimulation of getting out and keeping in touch with the thinking world (1 and 7). I'm doing a franchise-management course by correspondence. Some of the work involves computer searches, for marketing surveys, but the library has proper on-line facilities which it provides free of charge for the 'unwaged' like me (4 and 10). I also take the opportunity to do a little bargain-hunting, especially on market days, for food.

12.30 pm   I'm home again for a very light lunch by myself, since the wife has hers at work. This is the window for me to send away any job applications I've gathered up in the library.

2.30 pm   The wife returns and I take myself off to the allotment in the car because it's too risky to leave tools in the hut there (8). This thieving is a serious matter which, as a member of the Allotments Committee, I'm going to raise with the police (7). Despite the vandalism, there's no doubt that the allotment makes a big contribution to our standard of living (9). I've so developed my gardening skills that I'm almost thinking of trying a small gardening-associated franchise (6). This hobby certainly keeps you on your toes. You have to think ahead constantly, but you are also often looking forward to some pleasurable event or experience of the eating kind (2). I've now thought up one or two dodges of my own to save on water and fertiliser, both precious commodities on the allotments (5). There's also no doubt that gardening, and especially the digging, helps to keep you in tip-top physical condition (3). And it helps on the mental health front. Although being unemployed is a humiliating and demoralising experience, when you get in tune with the gentle, seasonal patterns of vegetable growing, then the whole predicament seems to shrink somewhat, and merge into a less critical perspective. You get caught up in a bigger and more reassuring system of things, which gives you confidence in yourself (1 and 2).

4.45 pm   I arrive home. This is, give or take half an hour, about the time I would return from work, which is a comforting thought (1).

7.00 pm   The wife is a considerable badminton player and although I am a rabbit (perhaps more accurately, a giraffe) at badminton, I drive her to the leisure centre, where I pass a strenuous hour on its gym machines. I find that if I play some evening exercise (it's not badminton-dodging every night) then I sleep better. It's essential I do sleep well, to avoid after-midnight fretting (1).

10.00 pm   Usually we settle down at 10, although sometimes we watch television through our toes (4).

Sustaining one's self-esteem under these circumstances is a *total* process. All actions and thoughts have to be tied to aim, and continuously aim-referenced. Tim, unconsciously, but very skilfully, shapes his lifestyle along the following guidelines:

1. Maintain normal daily rhythms, e.g. waking, rising, going out, etc.
2. Stimulate forward thinking and vital anticipations.
3. Retain or recover physical fitness.
4. Maintain existing mental alertness.
5. Sustain or enhance creativity.
6. Set up or focus 'hobby-into-job' schemes.
7. Secure and, if possible, widen social and community relationships.
8. Retain role-rhythms (personal space, etc.) between you and family members.
9. See if you can generate new income or job opportunities.
10. Perfect new skills for future use.

BROODING

Brooding is the inability to suppress memory of remote or recent events which have damaged self-esteem. They are regularly rehearsed or analysed, usually with appropriate low mood accompaniments, and show consistent features amongst which are:

- a non-solutional tendency – the brooding does not provide any answers

- a distorted perspective, usually deeply self-orientated

- a considerable persistence; the brooding is difficult to shift

- a colouring ability; the brooding will draw in other related events and blacken them also

- a rewarding capacity; this is the paradoxical pleasure that gloomy thinking gives those who secretly believe they deserve to be punished.

A useful statement list might be:

- No matter how long I mull over it, I never seem to get any further.

- It's all connected with me and my reactions.

- Once I've started it's difficult to stop.

- If I don't watch it, I find other matters being brought in, and similarly mulled over.

- I half-enjoy it, and always have done.

These statements can be very useful in breaking-up brooding episodes. They can be written, or typed out, and then placed in some private place where they can be read whenever episodes of brooding occur.

Appendix 3

Relaxation and Pleasure

RELAXATION

Relaxation is undoubtedly one excellent way of neutralising or minimising mental health problems. It involves a progressive loosening of muscles, softening of posture and slowing of pace. It can be practised formally in group-relaxation sessions or informally in any convenient circumstance. It costs little but its benefits can be priceless.

Formal relaxation serves two purposes. First, in itself it yields valuable episodes of ease. Second it provides useful practice updates, sets and maintains standards and facilitates informal relaxation. Informal relaxation uses opportunities in everyday life; for example, it promotes sleep for sufferers from insomnia.

CUES FOR RELAXATION

Individuals respond to different types of cues – visual, heard or felt – or combinations of the three. These people can be called visualisers, audiles and tactiles.

Visualisers will require some tranquil scene, depicted pictorially or in reality, and audiles peaceful music or a steady, rhythmic noise. Tactiles enjoy holding, stroking or massage, or total skin-stimulation such as in warm baths. For generations, rhythmic rocking has been known as a relaxant technique.

Babies who are rocked respond with pleasure, their restlessness tapering into sleep, and rocking may be for them a reminder of the movements felt in the womb. Rocking-chair rocking is also traditional, but not so effective as hammock-swinging.

RELAXATION ROUTINES

1. Dominantly breathing

- Lie down, or sit slackly with legs outstretched, head forward, eyes half-closed. If using stimulus, lock onto stimulus picture, induce sound or provide touch.

- Breathe out, pause for two/three seconds, and feel for faint, tingling sensation in lower limbs and base of the spine. Indulge this sensation.

- Breathe in fairly deeply, expanding the abdomen.

- Breathe out, let the head fall further forward, and experience the tingling sensation again.

- Breathe in.

- Breathe out and let the wave of tingling relaxation seep through your legs to your toes.

- Breathe in.

- Breathe out, and let the wave of tingling relaxation sweep through your arms to your finger tips.

- This wave sensation should be swift, on the edge of faint pain, and it should suffuse the limbs.

- Continue sweeping the sensation through your limbs to the steady rhythm of your breathing.

2. A rhythmic visualising theme

- Lie down or sit slumped in a chair with head inclined forward, eyes half-closed. Visual stimulus is appropriate.

- Set a loud, slow ticking, alarm-clock or metronome nearby.

- Concentrate gently on the ticking.

- Visualise the image of a swinging pendulum and focus on the image.

- Centralise the pendulum image in the chest, swinging to and fro in the chest cavity.

- Continue focusing until the image can be 'felt' in the chest.

- Then extend the focus, and let the image swing out to the arms and fingers.

- Lead it down to the buttocks and legs.

3. Lifting and dropping

- Lie down or sit slackly in a chair with legs outstretched, head forward, eyes half-closed. Visual, auditory or tactile stimuli are appropriate, as selected.

- Lift the right forearm with a slack wrist about six inches, hold it for twelve seconds, and let it fall.

- Lift the left forearm with a slack wrist about six inches, hold it for twelve seconds, and let it fall.

- Lift the right leg, slightly bent at the knee, about six inches. Hold it for about nine seconds, and let it fall.

- Lift the left leg, slightly bent at the knee, six inches, hold it for about nine seconds, and let it fall.

- Raise the head at an eyes horizontal position. Hold an object (could be relaxation picture) in vision for approximately twelve seconds, let the head drop.

- Brace the mid-portion of the body to clear the bed or base of chair by about three inches, hold the position for six seconds and then drop back.

- Repeat the routine until an overall, heavy, relaxed sensation suffuses all the body.

4. Relaxation to a suggestion tape

Persuade a friend of the opposite sex with a good recording voice to tape the following:

'Why don't you just close your eyes, and settle back and let the world simply drift by. I used to go to the banks of the River Ouse when I was a child. It's the sleepiest, slowest, river in the country, winding through flat meadow land with its banks lined with old split willows. I used to fish and when I got bored, I'd lie back on the rough grass, just dreaming. Big clouds would drift by above me and the humming of the insects in the meadow would blend with the cluck of moorhens and the occasional splash of a fish. After a while I could pick out individual noises, the deeper quack of a duck and the distant murmur of water as it washed through the sluices of the weir downstream. Sometimes, far away, I'd hear the hum of a mowing machine. Even then, I was learning to become aware of my body and how it functioned. I noticed how my breathing quietened; how it became regular and deep. I could feel my heart going lub dup, lub dup and I observed that its beat slowed as I relaxed. It was amazing how loose and slack my body grew as the afternoon drifted on. At times I felt detached from my limbs and floating outside myself; almost as if I were a leaf moving gently downstream on the smooth dark surface of the Ouse. It was as if I had become part of a magic river running quietly through sunlit, fairy, timeless meadows, on, on, spreading wider, until it came finally to the open waters of the sea.'

There is a huge range of relaxation routines available and the four we have just described are only a small selection.

RELAXATION MUSIC AND OTHER STIMULI FOR AUDILES

Relaxation music must be slow, but not lethargic or depressive. Above all, the music must have depth and be memorable without being boring. A fresh appetite should be created by its opening chords, every session.

Making up your own tapes
It is essential that you record your own selection of musical excerpts for relaxation. The original albums are usually un- suitable, almost certainly containing passages of unrelaxing content or over-sustained themes. Bringing different excerpts together can also be a good method of keeping up stimulus interest.

Suggested music for relaxation
Daphnis and Chloe, 'Aubade' (Daybreak)
   (Ravel)
Pavane for a dead Infanta (Ravel)   Philips 462.8502
Nocturne No 7 'Nuage' (Debussy)
Emperor Concerto (Beethoven)   DG 447.4022
'Gymnopedies' (Satie)   EMI 573.1092
'Albatross' (Fleetwood Mac)   Sony 477.5122
'Once upon a time in the West'
   (Film music)   Silver Screen 47362
'Tranquillity' (various)   EMI 573.1092

Pictures and other considerations for visuals
Relaxation with the assistance of a picture introduces some problems. There is the common challenge of boredom and the special difficulty that several of the previous relaxation routines

ask for half-closed eyes. Both are taken care of in the following ways. A selection of suitable pictures should be available but it is essential to keep to one picture per session. This is because the stimulus to relaxation should be simple and consistent so as to build up the swiftest possible conditioning link.

- A good relaxation picture should be full of *potential* interest, with every detail capable of being reinterpreted and questioned.

- A good relaxation picture offers itself in two stages; first, as a cue to detach the viewer from disruptive reality and, second, to cause a narrowing-down of the visual field. This narrowing can be dramatic. A blackening of perception outside the frame of the picture can sometimes be experienced.

- A good relaxation picture is moderate-sized or, preferably, a slide projected onto a screen.

- A good relaxation picture is one sufficiently well lit to be studied with half-closed eyes and positioned at an angle which will allow it to be seen clearly from a relaxed stance.

- Pair-working on pictures can enhance their relaxant value. A picture may reach a stage of familiarity (i.e. little or no new items of relaxing interest may be discernable) and become boring and counter-relaxing. At this point it is well worthwhile pair-working the picture (examining it with another person) to see if new aspects can be discovered, offering fresh penetration. Try such tactics as:
  - speculation/identification with figures or objects in the picture
  - speculation on climatic changes and their effects on the picture
  - speculation on the mood and circumstances of the painter.

- Visuals may also relax with the stimulus of well-chosen, real-life views.

Tactile stimulation

Although there are different ways of organising the kinds of tactile stimulation to serve as efficient relaxation aids, warm baths are probably the most practical. A suitable checklist for the total stimulus experience might run as follows:

- Bathroom environment. Is it conducive to relaxation? Are the fittings pleasant to look at? Are the walls restful to observe?

- Bath comfort. Is it big enough? Are pads needed?

- Bath availability. Is the bath available without interruption for an extended period, say one hour?

- Continuous warmth level. Does the bath lose heat rapidly? If so, insulation is needed. Is the hot-water supply adequate?

- Do you have an alarm system to wake you, should you fall asleep?

- Can you replenish hot water without much disturbance or noise? Continuous trickle through a tube, under water, may be the answer.

THE PLEASURE TEST

In this test you will find six panels A, B, C, D, E, F. Each panel contains descriptions of six different pleasures. Complete the panels as instructed. *Do not worry about opportunity. Rank each pleasure 1–6 as though it were possible for you.* Do not turn over to the second sheet until you have completed all the tasks on the first.

Panel A	Rank	**Panel B**	Rank
Going swimming/riding/jogging	❏	Doing a crossword competition	❏
Writing something creative	❏	Throwing a party for colleagues	❏
Meeting friends	❏	Sketching out plans for a new hobby	❏
Building things	❏	Relaxing after a good meal	❏
Anticipating and enjoying sexual relations	❏	Helping out with household repairs	❏
Watching TV at home	❏	Playing team sports	❏

Panel C	Rank	**Panel D**	Rank
Attending a convention/ conference	❏	Sewing, embroidery leather work, carpentry	❏
Modelling in clay, wood/stone	❏	Luxuriating in the bath	❏
Sitting on the toilet, reading	❏	Chatting with the family	❏
Gardening/vegetable growing	❏	Going walking	❏
Playing squash/tennis/ badminton	❏	Studying for a part-time course	❏
Arguing with congenial companions	❏	Attending a football/ cricket/hockey match	❏

Panel E	Rank	**Panel F**	Rank
Feeling genuine physical fatigue	❏	Arriving home in the evening	❏
Going visiting with the family	❏	Doing physical exercises/ music and movement	❏
Going skiing/skating/ tobogganing	❏	Reading an interesting and demanding book	❏
Going to a concert or play	❏	Attending a branch/ ward/group meeting	❏
Meeting friends after work/church	❏	Handling a new business venture	❏
Starting off a local organisation	❏	Feeling my body challenge the elements	❏

Rank the items 1–6. Put numbers in the right-hand boxes. 1 for most pleasurable, 6 for least pleasurable. No ties. Then collect the ranks by panel and note them down in the framework. Note down ranks from A to F, starting at the asterisk and putting the leftover rankings in the top. Add up ranks across the frame and rank again.

Example
Ranking, say, for Panel E – written down in Framework E

1	2
4	3
2	5
3	6
5	1
6	4

PANELS FRAMEWORK

	A	B	C	D	E	F	TOTAL	FINAL RANK
P				·				
Int		*						
So			*					
C				*				
Se					*			
Do						*		

———add across———

Now we have completed and scored the test, it is revealed that we have collected up a final ranking on six pleasure categories, namely:

P – physical (delight in body activity)
Int – intellectual (enjoyment or mental pursuits)
So – social (love of friends)
C – creative (delight in creating)
Se – sensual (love of bodily pleasure)
Do – domestic (love of home)

This enables us to identify our top preference pleasure (in terms of fantasy/perfect circumstances) and judge its status. It is only, of course, a top ranking which may be closely followed by others; indeed the numerical gaps may not be wide. According to such groupings we gain a view of potential pleasure areas which may be expanded. We can also see how the high ranking is made up in terms of individual panel scores, which in itself is a bridge to further insight about our pleasure potentialities.

Satisfactions survey
Tick if satisfied with:

☐ my available energy

☐ my assisted/unassisted hearing and vision

☐ my sense of balance

☐ my physical appearance

☐ my digestive/eliminative processes

☐ my overall state of health

☐ my acceptance by colleagues at work

☐ my career progress by contrast with my abilities

☐ the work-demands made upon me

☐ the purpose and ethics of my work

☐ the financial rewards of my work

☐ my place in the scheme of life

☐ the fact of my creation

☐ my status as a child of God

☐ my sense of being or personhood

☐ the inevitability of my death

☐ my ease in fresh social situations

☐ my capacity to recapture old social skills

☐ my social competence

☐ my capacity to take decisions

- [ ] my verbal fluency
- [ ] the relevance and power of my established skills
- [ ] my non-verbal flexibility
- [ ] my short-term memory
- [ ] my long-term memory
- [ ] my capability for fresh learning
- [ ] my creativity and originality
- [ ] my present range of interests
- [ ] my capacity to orchestrate my interests
- [ ] the relevance of my current interests to future needs
- [ ] my relationship with my spouse
- [ ] my relationship with my parents
- [ ] my relationship with my children
- [ ] my relationship with my near relatives
- [ ] my relationship with my friends
- [ ] my relationship with my acquaintances
- [ ] my relationship with my colleagues/collaborators
- [ ] my relationship with my neighbours
- [ ] the immediate prospects of people and organisations dear to me
- [ ] the longer-term prospects of people and organisations dear to me
- [ ] my belief in the integrity of authority
- [ ] the truth of my childhood memories
- [ ] the accuracy of later memories
- [ ] the sharpness of my appetite for food
- [ ] my capacity to savour tastes or flavours
- [ ] my sense of smell

☐ my secret pleasures such as elimination, scratching, smelling myself

☐ the preliminary pleasures of sex

☐ the response of my sexual partner

☐ the quality and intensity of my sexual orgasm

☐ my sensitivity to beauty

☐ my appreciation of harmony in music/art

☐ my feeling for my surroundings

☐ my care for the present environment

☐ my concern for the future of the environment

☐ the immediate prospects of my life

☐ the longer-term prospects for myself

Pleasure recollection

Remembrance of past pleasure, however vague or nostalgic by contrast with present despair, can be of great significance in recreating a pleasurable future. If an experience has been pleasurable in the past then, despite the fact that current circumstances seem to prevent it being attractive now, the pleasure-promoter has an opportunity. *A past pleasure was not a pleasure for nothing.* It once possessed a positive attraction which chimed in closely with needs and traits. Some elements of its previous holding power or some practised features may remain, and with effort, skill and imagination, be as effective as ever.

Instrument
Enter recollections in appropriate column. There is full flexibility in possible wording:

Long Term	**Short Term**
I took pleasure in:	I took pleasure in:
(10 years ago)	(1 year ago) . . . .
. . . .	. . . .
. . . .	. . . .
. . . .	. . . .

(20 years ago) . . . .   (18 months ago) . . . .
. . . .
. . . .
. . . .

(30 years ago) . . . .   (2 years ago)   . . . .
. . . .
. . . .
. . . .

Questions: How do long term and short term pleasures compare? Can you rank your pleasures?

Pleasure recollection case history

In his tense and miserable state, Mike could recall very little of his past. But some memories stood out, albeit vaguely. There was the fishing, for instance. He could remember that as a teenager he had gone to the canal with a pack of sandwiches and a vacuum flask and spent the Saturday afternoons float-watching.

And then there had been politics in his twenties. At one point he had been asked to stand as a councillor (the youngest in the municipal elections) but the illness of his father had prevented this. He could recall all those hectic ward-meetings where issues of great local significance had been discussed and afterwards the adjournments to a local cafe where argument had raged over weak coffee.

He'd also had a powerful passion for music then. The big names had been Shostakovitch and Prokofiev, and Mike had travelled miles to listen to their music. He had also tried his hand at an instrument, the flute, but the landlady had made fun of his practising, so this had faded away.

Recalling these, he had to struggle to remember, accurately and truthfully, all the various parts to the pleasure, so clouded and distorted were they by the unhappiness of the present. However, Martin had expressed enthusiasm for fishing. Mike determined to sound him out with a view to tagging along.

Pleasure planning case history

The prospect of a concert was something that Meryl was not going to pass up but, if she were to extract the maximum pleasure from it, she knew she would have to do some preliminary work. The advertised programme contained several pieces by a composer new to her so she borrowed a representative set of his recorded works from the record section of the library, taking care not to cover the programme itself. By this means she hoped to be able not only to catch the freshness of the composer, but attune herself to his style. She read a little of his life-history also and began to see how he fitted into the political and social climate of his era. On the day of the concert she kept a level mood, and booked herself a late supper with a friend after the concert was over.

HOW TO USE THIS MATERIAL

- Read the notes material thoroughly, consider its implications and possibilities and project its insights into your predicament.

- Complete the satisfactions survey. This is a wide-ranging instrument, giving you the opportunity to create a base-line of gratification, and identify areas to explore.

- Complete the pleasure test and compare the results with the reality of your pleasure-seeking lifestyle. Areas of pleasure preference should be explored for opportunities for fresh experience.

- Complete the pleasure recollection instrument and think about it together with the case history and the previous instruments. Conclusions should be fed into pleasure planning.

- Study the pleasure planning case history and start your own comparable pleasure planning. If you keep up a daily record, then you will be able to judge the extent to which pleasure needs to be intensified to compensate for suffering.

Appendix 4

Suicidal Thinking

The philsopher Nietzsche wrote 'The thought of suicide has helped me through many a dark night'. Like several of his sayings, it is an obvious paradox which also incorporates a profound truth. Pondering about and even planning suicide, as distinct from openly threatening it, do not necessarily imply an intention to kill oneself. Very often the opposite is true; thinking about suicide prevents the act. How it does so is an intricate piece of psychological self-deception, very revealing of a depressive's state of mind. When such suicidal thinking is definitely preventive, there are two possible mechanisms in play; the first and simplest operates on a contingency basis. The worst has not yet befallen the suicide-pondering, even promising, sufferer but, when it does, the will and means are ready to hand. This is a comfort of a kind to the sufferer and keeps him or her propped-up, waiting for the worst, while at the same time ready to adjust events to keep the pretence sustained.

The second mechanism has a subtler action. Here the suicidal thinking is *a substitute for the act itself*, incorporating in fantasy terms all the pain, rage and guilt that it typically entails, and doing useful restraining work. Provided the depression is a steady state, why then should one kill oneself when all the psychological advantages of suicide are ready to hand and can be actively enjoyed?

Clearly these are the thought-patterns of poorly-motivated, suicide-considerers. So what might characterise the thinking of those who actually *do* kill themselves?

The short answer is, we do not know, but we hedge around a few tentative hypotheses. Some assumptions are:

1. Thoughts are characterised by a very strong rage or revenge elements.
2. 'Window-thinking' e.g. the timing of opportunistic suicide becomes dominant.

3. Pledges of suicide are given, e.g. threats to commit the act are openly voiced to others.
4. Impulse fantasies of violent action are common, and very pleasurable.
5. Peace fantasies are similarly frequent and intense.

Almost all persons at some time in their lives become preoccupied with suicidal thoughts, particularly if they are experiencing depressive episodes. As we have emphasised, such thoughts can usually be classified as expected or perhaps preventive. If, however, you are very depressed and experience any of the assumptions 1–5, then *you may be a serious suicide risk, and should seek medical help*.

Assumption 3 is of special significance, because it is the only one of the five that can alert one to the suicidal urges of another person. Unfortunately, it is commonly considered to be a sign that the pledge-giver, or threatener will *not* commit suicide. This is a profound mistake; those who threaten sometimes do. So take threats made by others seriously, and obtain swift professional help for them.

Appendix 5

Leisure Counselling

What is leisure counselling? It is a general term for strategies that use hobbies, activities or interests (HAI) for specific therapeutic purposes. There are three conventional modes.

Distraction This is when the HAI is employed to shift attention away from a sufferer's pain, problem or symptom.

Compensation Here the HAI acts as a mental balance-weight in an imaginative sense against depressing or anxiety-creating circumstances.

Confrontation In this mode the HAI's characteristics directly challenge the problem on its own ground, forcing it in the best case to relax its grip and psychological influence.

Leisure counselling is *a supplementary therapy*, not employed in isolation, but as part of a wider therapeutic scheme.

CASE HISTORY

Melissa is depressed

Melissa is 37, separated and childless. Her life has fallen apart; her personal relationships have failed and her attitudes and mood are bitter and suicidal. Indeed she has already made one suicide attempt: a half-hearted effort with about 20 aspirins which put her to sleep for about five hours and left her feeling sick. By some freak of fortune, she still has a part-time job, but it's meaningless and futile employment, apart from the money. Melissa's ex-husband never wanted a family, insisting that they 'get themselves firmly established first,' but that achieved, he took himself off.

Mornings are the worst. Sometimes she will lie awake for hours before the alarm goes, fretting about her future. She's hardly got the motivation to brush her hair, and Melissa's hair is her finest asset. Cooking for one is no thrill, so she misses out on breakfast, has a roll for lunch and a take-away most nights. Her mood is black for much of the day; thoughts of personal inadequacy bug her; she is burdened by overwhelming problems and duties, and seems incapable of sustaining anything more than superficial personal relationships. Constantly, she ruminates over past mistakes; why did she not marry the man she was engaged to before she met her ex? Why did she marry at all?

Melissa's father is dead and her mother, somewhat demoralised, is living in sheltered accommodation, so there is no residual childhood home still available. She's an only child as well, with distant cousins as extended family, and where she presently lives is where she was transplanted by her ex, 50 miles from where she was born.

The counsellor in her case, faced with this serious problem of social isolation and lack of appropriate re-attachment skills, pesuades her to consider amateur drama with a local society. In terms of mode this interest combines elements of compensation and confrontation with the emphasis on the former.

There are at least nine possible benefits, perhaps more, in amateur drama for Melissa. She may:

- gain practice in verbal/non verbal communication skills

- make fresh social contacts

- meet needs for self-dramatisation

- discover personal interpretation and resolution of conflicts via dramatic themes

- find particular roles of great cathartic value in, for example, acting-out impulses

- gain general confidence from the perfection of dramatic skills

- break typical ruminative sequences or thought-routines of self-denigration

- be compelled to adopt better grooming habits

- have rehearsal and performance as positive anticipation opportunities.

Amateur drama is not, of course, Melissa's exclusive HAI; it is, however, one which reflects her interests, needs and circumstances as agreed between her and the counsellor.

Let us now assume that Melissa is well into her counselling programme and is keeping up a daily chart including all the action sites. Her notes clearly show that she is integrating the amateur drama in at least three Action Site modes.

Daily Chart

	Success Rating
1. *Waking thoughts and feelings* I got up at 6.45 and went for a fifteen minute jog, not forgetting to take my personal alarm.	B
2. *Routine depressive events* Managed to get out of the house before the mail arrived. Will face it later when I'm stronger!	B
3. *Other upsets* Used thought-stopping to block a sudden thought that I might dry-up at the next rehearsal.	B
4. *Relationships* Made a fresh contact in the general audit department.	B
5. *Appetite* They've opened a marvellous delicatessen round the corner, which I'm going to patronise.	A
6. *Upswings* Felt more cheerful after lunch. On the strength managed to sell two tickets for the spring play to a visitor.	B
7. *Looking forward* For the first time managed to get word perfect on my part in Act Two.	A
8. *Reinforcements* Booked myself a holiday at Whitsun, so that I can anticipate it.	A
9. *Unconscious mind* Ran my nagging-mum tape twice and really shouted the retorts.	B
10. *Sleeping and presleeping* Went through the routines faithfully, and woke up only once during the night.	B

Looked at in greater psychological detail her interest may be expected to yield the following:

Cognitive/Behavioural benefits of the developed interest

- **Skills (social, emotional, technical) which will undermine the ailment**
  Dress, grooming and conversational skills have all developed from the, as yet, limited stage performance and show promise of further gain. Friends have noted she is more poised.

- **Secondary gains (social, financial, material) which will strengthen the interest**
  Financial/material gains are nil; but a thriving social circle has developed around the drama group, and there may be opportunity to make deeper relationships with some members.

- **Anticipation potential – degree of anticipated pleasure expected from the interest**
  There is certainly opportunity for pleasure-scheduling. Part-study, rehearsals and performances all encourage this and are stimulus points for anticipations.

- **Masking – activities within the interest generating fatigue/ excitement, etc, calculated to starve or crowd depression**
  The excitement and tension of rehearsal and actual performance are quite sufficient to break up the rhythm of the depression cycle.

- **Desensitisation – selective experiences within the interest tending to neutralise fears, etc.**
  Conquering stage-fright is an empowering experience and gives promise of mastery of other feelings.

- **Reciprocal-inhibition – ailment fantasies or behaviour acted out safely in interest, thus inhibiting real-life symptoms**
  The part calls for her to run around, distracted, on the stage. She used to behave this way in private at home, but since the acting-out experience, the pressure has lessened.

- **Aversion – aspects of the interest totally incompatible with the ailment**
  It is impossible to be depressed and to act a lively part and thus a strong, occasional, aversion element has emerged in the interest.

- **Reinforcement – aspects of the interest that strengthen the client's defences against depression**
  She is certainly making a success of her part which encourages a sense of self-worth and value to others.

Thus leisure counselling has produced a supplementary but powerful, therapeutic lever by searching out available client and local resources.

For explanations of the technical terms employed in this case history, see the appendix on cognitive-behavioural psychology.

Appendix 6

Cognitive-behavioural psychology and depression

As we have emphasised throughout the book, depression is a slippery, changeable entity not easy to grip, influence or modify. The self-manager needs suitable tools which can be supplied by cognitive-behavioural psychology. Equipped with these, direct attempts may be made to adjust thinking, feeling and action, and so gain an advantage over the depressive state.

EIGHT TOOLS TO TACKLE SYMPTOMS

A symptom can be:

- an idea

- an action, willed or compelled

- a feeling, describable or indescribable

- a reflex, such as an immediate, involuntary response.

A symptom may be:

- **relabelled**, usually to minimise its significance and thus isolate it

- **ignored** e.g. crowded out by other thoughts and thus diminished

- **extinguished** by punishment or aversive conditioning

- **encouraged**, i.e. caused to present itself on or off schedule and thus exhaust itself

- **recorded**, and thus, mysteriously, diminish in frequency

- **conditioned** to its disadvantage, i.e. forced to coexist with antagonistic, powerful, counter-ideas, actions or feelings and thus, squeezed

- **confronted** and broken by an act of will

- **substituted for**, intentionally or accidentally by a less painful, more practical idea, action or feeling.

Relabelling This is justifiably at the head of the list, since its applicability is great. Notable amongst strategies developed with it are:

- **Relabelling**, the deliberate attempt to substitute more neutral adjectives or terms for emotionally provoking thoughts or self-statements.

- **Counter-philosophising**, identifying classes of thoughts by reference to learned, maladaptive habits of thinking, e.g. the habit of over-emphasising response to events, 'catastrophising'. Counter-philosophising attacks such habits.

- **Straight-thinking**, the attack on dubious conclusions from shaky or ambiguous facts, e.g. imagining a slight or insult where the intent was not clear and might have been misinterpreted.

- **Thought-stopping**, identifying trains of self-derogatory thinking, either event-responsive or automatic, which can and should be stopped before they rouse inappropriate feelings.

- **Positive thinking practice**, the most forceful emphasis on positive, planful thinking, thinking positively in every working moment and rewarding yourself for excluding negative thoughts.

Extinguishing This is an inappropriate cognitive-behavioural tool for depression which in itself is often a response to punishment or aversive circumstances. However, electro-convulsive shock therapy seems to 'extinguish' depression thus.

Encouraging There have been attempts made to use this tool; in the deliberate, almost provocative prompting of a self-denigrating thought to repeat itself ad infinitum, and thereby *exhaust its capacity to generate a self-depreciatory mood*. But this may be a self-defeating tactic.

Recording This is a tool with several uses; we can employ it to judge progress, assess strategy-success and remotivate ourselves. It also often has a semi-automatic, ameliorative effect, at least initially, which can be observed soon after recording begins.

Conditioning Breaking the conditioning link which causes a symptom to emerge on cue, or building up a connection between an event and a positive mood, are typical examples of conditioning in action. It is a very useful and multi-purpose tool.

Confronting There are various aspects to confrontation, all of which depend on the cognitive-behavioural axiom '*Behaving is becoming*'. Within these it is possible to train oneself first to *act* cheerful, and then to *be* cheerful as a consequence. Examples of direct aspects are to be found in laughter therapy for depression by which induced laughter encourages deeper breathing and provides a natural high by increasing the supply of confidence-making neuro-chemicals in the brain. Humour and laughter clubs can also be formed for depressives, where a variety of films and tapes are played to encourage cheerful responses.

Examples of indirect aspects are found in leisure counselling contexts where those whose depressions are, for instance, dependent on social isolation and lack of social skills, find themselves in situations where they have to interact with others.

Substituting Symptoms in this area usually present themselves as unresolved or unsatisfied needs which react against the self by downgrading and demoralising attacks on appearance, achievements, etc. However, if such needs can be recognised and realistic substitute ideas or activities found for them, then much depression-creating backlash can be avoided altogether or its effects minimised.

Suggested Reading

Dealing with depression, Trevor Barnes (Vermilion, 1996)

Depression: the commonsense approach, Tony Bates (Newleaf, Dublin, 1999)

How to accept yourself, Windy Dryden (Sheldon, 1999)

Manual for leisure-counselling, Dean Juniper (Kirkfield, 1994)

Break free from depression, and let your feelings out, Marie Langley (Unwind, 1997)

Understanding depression, Liz Maclaren (Brockhampton Press, 1996)

Anxiety and depression, Robert Priest (Vermilion, 1996)

Depression: the way out of your prison, Dorothy Rowe (Routledge, 1996)

Malignant sadness: the anatomy of depression, Lewis Wolpert (Faber & Faber, 1999)

Useful Addresses

Depression Alliance, 35 Westminster Bridge Rd, London SE1 7JB.

Fellowship of Depressives Anonymous, 36 Chestnut Avenue, Beverley HV17 9QU.

Manic-Depression Fellowship, 8–10 High St, Kingston-on-Thames, Surrey KT1 1EY.

Samaritans: check for local number.

Sane, 2nd Floor 199–205 Old Marylebone Rd, London NW1 5QP.

Index